Monastic

jovis

Monastic

Friederike von Rauch

jovis

“Darkness Is My Solution.”

Spatial Experience in the Photographs of Friederike von Rauch

Friederike von Rauch's spaces are deserted, sheltering what is a rare and precious commodity these days: silence. Time can be felt with your eyes in them. Light takes shape in frequently subdued hues that appear all the more intense against the darkness, leading surfaces to shimmer or shine, no matter how angular, rough, faded, weathered, or fragmented they may be. Every single moment photographed by von Rauch, and the gaze captured within it—whether directed outwards or inwards—is condensed in the velvety, fragile texture of the pigment prints, which bring out the specific pictorial character of these analog shots.

Reduced to exclusively square formats in a few fixed dimensions dictated by the motif, the works are decidedly focused, concentrating in detail on the light as it falls, so as to detect those tracks quietly leading from darkness to light, where secrets are at home and their effects unfold in every direction: spatially, temporally, contemplatively, even spiritually, though each element is very much of this world. In analogy to light and darkness, knowledge and intimation are anchored in the picture, and closely interwoven with the motif. Is it so important to possess certainty, to grasp everything down to the smallest grain? Barely registered, the bright light will leave new traces in the darkness and direct our attention to other areas.

Von Rauch's subtle sensitivity for the individual character of a place can be seen in all of her pictures, be they nameless buildings, barely noticed spatial arrangements, or the well-known, representative interiors of museums and sacred buildings familiar from architectural and cultural history and now largely accessible to the public. To open up these spaces in ways that go beyond what has been seen hitherto, to display them in palpably new ways and focus on the sensory allure of even the most minor details, to open up proportions and materiality, not least with light and shadow, and in all of this to allow the unfathomable to be experienced—this is the peculiar strength of her photographs.

Von Rauch's extensive journeying began at the turn of the millennium with some of Berlin's hidden places, which became widely visible thanks, not least, to her photographs; they led her from the German metropolis to architecturally similar views in other parts of Europe, especially closely related contemporary spots in Brussels and Rotterdam. She refers to these scenes of modernity and so-called Brutalism simply as “sites,” photographed in broad daylight, in nocturnal light, or in a darkness illuminated by daylight: factual, cool, reduced, brittle, often spanned by a monochrome, light gray sky that, when the picture was taken, immersed everything in foggy white light and gave it an air of unreality. In the middle of the series, windows opened up onto industrial landscapes whose imperfections and inscribed structures made it possible to guess at their origins and use or displayed the consequences of natural events—but without revealing a single trace of any human beings. Each picture logged a state of affairs: detailed, naturalistic, and yet peculiarly remote from reality.

To this day, the path to these photos can be long and, over time, often lonely. The initial idea is followed by research, interviews, permits, and longer stays or recurring visits. These form the prelude to every series of photos, and at the end of this process only a few uncompromisingly selected situations, where the light and the atmosphere are just right, live up to the artist's unerring sense of the radiance of different spaces. Her choice of places and buildings over the last two decades ranges from publicly accessible urban spaces in which transitory situations are seen—temporary residences or shelters caught at some point between the presence and absence of their (former) inhabitants or users—to representative museum areas, which are also transitory spaces with changing visitors and presentations.

„Die Dunkelheit ist meine Lösung.“

Raumerfahrung in den Fotografien von Friederike von Rauch

Ihre Räume sind menschenleer. Sie bergen eine selten gewordene, kostbare Stille. Zeit ist mit den Augen zu ertasten. Licht nimmt Gestalt an in vielfach gedämpften Farbtönen, die aus dem Dunkel umso intensiver aufscheinen und Oberflächen zum Schimmern oder Leuchten bringen, seien sie auch noch so kantig, rau, verblichen, verwittert oder fragmentiert. Jeder einzelne von Friederike von Rauch fotografierte Moment und der darin festgehaltene Blick – ob nach außen oder nach innen gerichtet – verdichtet sich in der samtig-fragilen Textur der Pigmentdrucke, die den spezifischen Bildcharakter dieser analogen Aufnahmen untermalen.

Reduziert auf ausschließlich quadratische Formate in wenigen festgelegten, an das Motiv gebundenen Maßen, zeigen sich die Werke entschieden fokussiert, konzentrieren sich detailgenau auf einfallendes Licht, um jene leisen Spuren zwischen Hell und Dunkel zu finden, in dem das Geheimnis zu Hause ist und seine Wirkung in jedwede Richtung entfaltet: räumlich, zeitlich, kontemplativ, auch spirituell und mit jedem Baustein doch ganz und gar weltlich. In Analogie zu Licht und Dunkel sind Wissen und Ahnung im Bild verankert und zeigen sich auf das Engste mit dem Motiv verwoben. Ist es von Belang, Gewissheit zu haben und alles bis auf das kleinste Korn zu durchdringen? Kaum erfasst, wird der helle Schein neue Spuren in die Dunkelheit legen und die Achtsamkeit auf andere Bereiche lenken.

Das feine Gespür für die Besonderheit eines Ortes zeigt sich in allen Bildern der Künstlerin – seien es namenlose Architekturen, kaum beachtete räumliche Situationen oder weithin bekannte repräsentative, museale und sakrale Innenräume der Architektur- und Kulturgeschichte, die heute in großen Teilen der Öffentlichkeit zugänglich sind. Diese über das bisher Gesehene hinaus in sensibel erfassten Ausschnitten neu zu öffnen, den sinnlichen Reiz auch noch so nebensächlicher Details aufzuspüren, Proportionen und Materialität nicht zuletzt mit Licht und Schatten zu erschließen und in allem auch Unergründliches erfahrbar werden zu lassen, ist allen Fotografien von Friederike von Rauch zu eigen.

Begonnen hat die raumgreifende Reise um die Jahrtausendwende mit verborgenen Orten in Berlin, die nicht zuletzt durch Friederike von Rauchs Aufnahmen weithin sichtbar wurden und sie aus der deutschen Metropole zu bauzeitlich kompatiblen europäischen, durchaus verwandten Ansichten in Brüssel und Rotterdam führten. Schlicht „Sites“ bezeichnet sie diese Schauplätze der Moderne und des sogenannten Brutalismus, aufgenommen am helllichten Tag, bei Nachthelle oder in taghell ausgeleuchteter Dunkelheit: sachlich, kühl, reduziert, spröde, oft überspannt von einem monochromen lichtgrauen Himmel, der beim Entstehen des Bildes alles in nebelweißes Licht tauchte und der Realität entrückte. Inmitten der Serie öffneten sich Fenster in industriell geprägte Landschaftsräume, deren Fehlstellen und eingeschriebene Strukturen Rückschlüsse auf die Entstehung und Nutzung ermöglichen oder die Folgen von Naturereignissen greifbar machen – ohne auch nur eine Spur von Menschen zu offenbaren. Jedes Bild ein Zustandsprotokoll: detailliert, naturalistisch und doch der Wirklichkeit eigentümlich fern.

Es ist bis heute ein langer und auf weite Strecken auch einsamer Weg zu diesen Fotografien. Der Idee folgen Recherchen, Gespräche, Genehmigungen und längere Aufenthalte oder wiederkehrende Besuche. Sie bilden das Entrée einer jeden Werkreihe, an deren Ende nur wenige, kompromisslos ausgewählte, vom Licht geführte und von der Atmosphäre getragene Situationen dem untrüglichen Gespür der Künstlerin für die Ausstrahlung von Räumen standhalten. Betrachtet man rückblickend die Wahl der Orte und Architekturen der letzten zwei Jahrzehnte, entspinnt sich ein loser Faden vom öffentlich zugänglichen Stadtraum, darin gesehenen Durchgangssituationen mit

Making this aspect of the transient scene visible and capturing it in a picture—especially in the context of collections aimed at conservation, or in listed buildings—is something that can be achieved in a characteristic and special way when a place is undergoing restoration or reorganization, which gives the photographer an unobstructed and at the same time private and intimate view of the inner lives of these spaces and their constant transformation. The precise photographic records she made during the restoration of the Neues Museum (New Museum) in Berlin or the incomparable scenes she discovered during her forays behind the scenes in the Neues Palais (New Palace) in Potsdam also capture the smallest details, opening windows into time with a gaze both sympathetic and incorruptible. What she fixes in her images ranges from close detail to the comprehensive experience of space, with light made visible and proportions laid bare.

From these views of the nonpublic sphere of a museum whose job it is to foster intense perception and specialized knowledge, it was only a small step to selected churches and monasteries, where, in seclusion and silence, she could more broadly and deeply trace the intellectual as well as the sensual and (for both visitors and residents) spiritual fusion of architecture, space, and light, and record it adequately in her photos.

The first monastery photographed by von Rauch was Neviges, the architectural jewel designed by Gottfried Böhm. As a place of pilgrimage, the building still attracts not only the faithful, but all those interested in architecture, with its sculptural structures on a polygonal floor plan. Following the traces of light and shadow on a rugged gray stone, immersed in the deepest darkness, a disbeliever filled with wonder, she experienced a deep faith inside this "rough diamond," as she described the site. In the resulting photographs, the place seems less unreal than uncanny—an earthen house of concrete and paved structures, offset by candles that create more shadows than light.

Her next destination was La Tourette, near Lyon. Here for the first time she lived and worked in a monastery. "The thought of living in a building by Le Corbusier appealed to me.... I could wander around, observe the light, observe myself, too, without having to hurry. I could always react, or not—at night, in the afternoon, for ten minutes, or not at all," wrote von Rauch in her diarylike notes.[1] She took the time to experience the building, which is as monumental as it is light and diaphanous in its architectural structures. Soon, as had already been the case in other, secular spaces, she was given carte blanche to take photographs in the church and the crypt, even in the dark. Only when completely undisturbed could she avoid the "extreme shades of color that Corbusier used here. The darkness is my solution. Time works to my advantage"—this was her logical conclusion. Yet the moonlight surprised her. It cast a "strange coolness over Le Corbusier's light shafts over the crypt with its many altars" and gave a characteristic tonality to her shots of the interior, captured in all their light and color, both clear and schematic in outline. On the other hand, the view into the surrounding countryside, through the vertical struts of the windows rhythmically arranged by Iannis Xenakis, is rain-misted and completely opaque: some secrets remain impenetrable—even by day.

In Berlin, she visited the memorial church and convent of Maria Regina Martyrum, where she encountered nuns for the first time. In the starkly reduced and abstracted photographs that she took there, the perfect beauty of the rough concrete is revealed, shining and shimmering in places, transforming the church with its signs of aging into a precious gem that makes one forget the size and simplicity of the building.

Her visit to Roosenberg, another convent, resulted in monastic views that are characterized by warmth and materiality—intensified by the

1 This and the following quotations are taken from the unpublished notes the photographer took on her visits to various monasteries between 2013 and 2018.

temporär genutzten Aufenthalts- oder Schutzräumen – festgehalten irgendwo zwischen An- und Abwesenheit seiner (einstigen) Bewohner oder Nutzer – hin zu repräsentativen musealen Orten, ebenfalls transitorische Räume mit wechselnden Besuchern und Präsentationen.

Diesen Aspekt des Flüchtigen – gerade im Kontext konservierender Sammlungsbestände und denkmalgeschützter Architekturen – sichtbar zu machen und im Bild zu bewahren, gelingt auf charakteristische und besondere Weise im Zuge von Erneuerungen oder Umordnungen, die der Fotografin einen unverstellten und gleichsam privaten, intimen Blick auf das Innenleben der Räume und ihren steten Wandel ermöglichen. Die präzisen fotografischen Aneignungen während der Wiederherstellung des Neuen Museum in Berlin oder die unnachahmlichen Einblicke während ihrer Streifzüge hinter die Kulissen im Neuen Palais in Potsdam halten auch kleinste Zeitfenster mit so einfühlsamen wie unbestechlichen Blicken fest. Immer lässt sich ein Bogen spannen von detailreicher Nahsichtigkeit bis zur umfassenden Raumerfahrung, mit gesehenem Licht und vorgefundener Proportion ausschnitthaft ins Bild gesetzt.

Von diesen Einsichten in den nichtöffentlichen Bereich einer der intensiven Wahrnehmung und Erkenntnis dienenden musealen Institution war es nur ein kleiner Schritt hin in ausgewählte Kirchenräume und Klosteranlagen, um in Abgeschiedenheit und Stille der so sinnigen wie sinnlichen und in den Augen der Besucher und Bewohner nicht zuletzt auch spirituellen Verschmelzung von Architektur, Raum, Licht weiter und tiefer nachzuspüren und eine Entsprechung in den Fotografien zu finden.

Das erste Kloster, das Friederike von Rauch fotografierte, war Neviges, architektonisches Juwel von Gottfried Böhm und Pilgerstätte. Der Bau lockt bis heute nicht nur Gläubige, sondern an Architektur Interessierte mit seinen skulpturalen Strukturen auf polygonalem Grundriss. Den Spuren von Licht und Schatten auf graurauem Stein folgend, eingetaucht in tiefste Dunkelheit, erlebt sie, ungläubig staunend, tiefen Glauben im Innern dieses „Rohdiamants“, als der ihr der Ort erscheint. Weniger unwirklich denn unwirtlich zeigt sich das Haus in den dort entstandenen Fotografien – ein irdisches Gehäuse aus Beton und gepflasterten Strukturen, versetzt mit Kerzen, die mehr Schatten als Licht erzeugen.

Das nächste Ziel ist La Tourette nahe Lyon. Hier wohnt und arbeitet sie erstmals in einem Kloster. „In einer Corbusier-Architektur zu wohnen, hat mich gereizt. (...) Umherwandeln, Licht beobachten, mich selbst auch, ohne Eile. Immer reagieren können, oder eben auch nicht. Nachts, nachmittags, für zehn Minuten, gar nicht“,[1] hält Friederike von Rauch in tagebuchartigen Notizen fest. Sie lässt sich Zeit, diesen äußerlich so monumentalen wie in seinen architektonischen Strukturen lichten und durchlässigen Gebäudekomplex zu erfahren. Bald bekommt sie, wie bereits an anderen weltlichen Orten, eine Carte blanche, um völlig ungestört in der Kirche und in der Krypta auch bei Dunkelheit fotografieren zu können. Nur so kann sie die „extremen Farbtöne, die Corbusier hier benutzt hat, umgehen. Die Dunkelheit wird meine Lösung. Die Zeit spielt für mich“, ist ihre logische Schlussfolgerung. Dennoch: Das Mondlicht überrascht sie. Es wirft „diese seltsame Kühle über Corbusiers Lichtschächte auf der Krypta mit den vielen Altären“ und wird kennzeichnend für die ausschnitthaften, von Licht und Farbe so klar wie schemenhaft gezeichneten Innenansichten. Der Blick in die umgebende Natur durch die von Iannis Xenakis rhythmisierten vertikalen Fensterstreben dagegen zeigt sich regenverhangen und gänzlich opak: Geheimnisse bleiben undurchdringlich – auch bei Tage.

In Berlin wird die Gedenkkirche mit Kloster Maria Regina Martyrum Aufenthaltsort und erste Begegnung mit Ordensfrauen. In den dort

1 Dieses und folgende Zitate nach unveröffentlichten Aufzeichnungen der Künstlerin zu ihren Klosterreisen 2013 bis 2018.

windows that look out onto the snowy landscape—and lend a unique vigor to the finely balanced proportions and vistas of the architecture by Dom Hans van der Laan. "A dream of color and material.… Perhaps this is the most contemplative place on my monastery journeys," wrote von Rauch in her notes, actually revealing much more about human encounters and related stories than about the architectural experiences of her monastery visits. Here, near Antwerp, she experienced a living sense of order and structures that shape every day; all this is echoed in her photographs of the monastery complex. This complex was closed soon after her stay and is presently seeking new residents and a suitable function.

The final destination of von Rauch's monastic journey depicted in this volume was in Italy. Her stay at the monastery of San Giorgio Maggiore in Venice combined seclusion and insularity with the balanced proportions of Andrea Palladio's seminal buildings, which pay homage to models of antiquity. They provide a grandiose foil, enabling us to see color and light in a completely different way from the previously visited monasteries of the north. Here, the tone is set by painters, especially those whose works can be viewed in the monastery: Vittore Carpaccio and, above all, Tintoretto. The surrounding water of the lagoon city always joins in with its gently shimmering nuances. The color shines out in a beguiling red that reverberates in the tightly woven canvas, covering a niche, dampening the sound, and outshining the watery, gray-white walls that here alone, in this special light, can gracefully age. "Shadows, lights, edges, textures, colors, breath"—this, in a nutshell, is the essence of her memories of her time here, so close to the bustling city and yet far away from the streaming crowds of people, in a dreamlike and yet perfectly real place.

In all the photographs in von Rauch's Monastic series, shot between 2013 and 2018 in five different monasteries, her reduced, sensual images once again form an incomparable symbiosis of the power of unexpected moments, material allure, and the individual experience of light and space. As Donald Judd put it, "Proportion is very important to us, both in our minds and lives and as objectified visually, since it is thought and feeling undivided, since it is unity and harmony, easy or difficult, and often peace and quiet. Proportion is specific and identifiable in art and architecture and creates our space and time."[2] Friederike von Rauch builds on these foundations with color and materiality; she paints with light. With her photographs she evokes an inimitable sound of silence, a singular moment that echoes again and again as we gaze at her pictures.

Birgit Möckel

2 Donald Judd, "Art and Architecture" (1983), in *Res: Anthropology and Aesthetics* 7/8 (Spring/Fall 1984): 147–54, http://x-arch.blogspot.com/2005/11/donald-judd-art-and-architecture.html.

entstandenen, stark reduzierten und abstrahierten Fotografien zeigt sich der raue Beton in vollendeter Schönheit, glänzt und schimmert partiell und lässt den Kirchenraum mit seinen Alterungsspuren als kostbares Kleinod erscheinen, das die Größe und Schlichtheit des Baus vergessen macht.

Mit einem Besuch in Roosenberg, auch dies ein Frauenkloster, nehmen – intensiviert durch Fensterblicke in die verschneite Landschaft – Wärme und Stofflichkeit Einzug in die Fotografien und geben den fein austarierten Proportionsideen und Blickachsen des Architekten Dom Hans van der Laan eine in dieser „Monastic"-Serie einmalige lebendige Kraft. „Ein Traum an Farbe und Material (…). Möglicherweise ist das der kontemplativste Ort meiner Klosterreisen", so konstatiert Friederike von Rauch in ihren Erinnerungen, die im Grunde weit mehr von den menschlichen Begegnungen und dazugehörigen Geschichten, denn von den Architekturerfahrungen ihrer Klosterbesuche erzählen. Hier, bei Antwerpen, erfährt sie gelebte Ordnung und alltägliche, ordnende Strukturen, die ihr Echo in den Aufnahmen dieser kurz nach ihrem Aufenthalt verlassenen Klosteranlage finden, die heute nach neuen Inhalten und damit verbundenen Botschaften sucht.

Der Schlusspunkt der in diesem Band publizierten „monastischen Reise" wird in Italien gesetzt. Mit dem Aufenthalt im Kloster San Giorgio Maggiore in Venedig verknüpfen sich Abgeschiedenheit und Insellage mit den an der Antike orientierten ausgewogenen Proportionen der wegweisenden Bauten von Andrea Palladio. Eine grandiose Folie, um Farbe und Licht völlig anders zu sehen als in den bisher besuchten Klöstern des Nordens. Hier setzen Maler, insbesondere die, deren Werke im Kloster zu erleben sind, den Ton: Vittore Carpaccio und allen voran Tintoretto. Und das alles umgebende Wasser der Lagunenstadt spielt mit sanft schillernden Schattierungen immer mit. Die Farbe leuchtet in einem betörenden Rot, das im dichtgewebten Tuch nachwirkt, wenn es eine Nische verhüllt, den Klang dämpft und die wässrig grauweißen Wände überstrahlt, die nur dort, nur bei diesem Licht mit Anmut altern. „Schatten, Licht, Kanten, Texturen, Farben, Hauch", lesen sich kurz gefasst und auf ihre Essenz verknappt die Erinnerungen an diesen Aufenthalt ganz nahe der quirligen Stadt und doch weit weg von den Menschenströmen – an einem unwirklichen und gleichwohl ganz realen Ort.

In all ihren zwischen 2013 und 2018 in den fünf so unterschiedlichen Klöstern entstandenen Fotografien der Reihe „Monastic" finden die reduzierten, sinnlichen Bilder von Friederike von Rauch einmal mehr zu einer unvergleichlichen Symbiose aus der Kraft unerwarteter Momente, stofflichem Reiz und dem individuellen Erleben von Licht und Raum. „Proportion ist für uns sehr wichtig, sowohl in unserem Denken und Leben als auch visuell umgesetzt, denn in ihr sind Denken und Fühlen nicht voneinander getrennt, sie ist Einheit und Harmonie, einfach oder schwierig und oft Frieden und Ruhe. In der Kunst und in der Architektur ist Proportion spezifisch und identifizierbar, sie schafft uns Zeit und unseren Raum", resümiert Donald Judd in seinen hinterlassenen Schriften.[2] Friederike von Rauch erweitert diese Grundfesten um Farbe und Materialität, gemalt mit Licht. Sie evoziert mit ihren Fotografien einen unnachahmlichen Klang von Stille als singulären Moment, der wieder und wieder anklingt beim Betrachten ihrer Bilder.

Birgit Möckel

2 Donald Judd: „Kunst und Architektur" (1983), in: ders.: *Architektur*, Stuttgart 1992, S. 143–145, hier: S. 143.

La lumière au couvent de La Tourette

Vivre au couvent de La Tourette, c'est habiter un lieu spirituel, œuvre architecturale construite par Le Corbusier pour les Dominicains aux environs de Lyon à la fin des années cinquante. Il est l'écrin aujourd'hui de la vie religieuse d'une communauté d'une dizaine de frères dominicains.
Pour Le Corbusier l'architecture est le jeu correct et savant de volumes assemblés sous la lumière. Il aimait dire aux frères qu'il avait construit l'église du couvent avec deux matériaux : le béton et la lumière. La lumière est un élément central dans l'architecture de Le Corbusier qui la met en scène et qui étudie la façon dont elle pénètre les volumes.
Nous sommes touchés par la rigueur des formes architecturales. L'harmonie des volumes et l'équilibre des proportions agissent sur nous. Le Corbusier parle d'un espace indicible. Pas de décoration, pas de distraction visuelle, rien de superflu. Par une économie de moyens, nous sommes conduits à l'essentiel. Cela nous apprend à voir, à contempler, notamment les jeux d'ombre et de lumière sur les murs. Sous la lumière changeante, les murs et les sols se transforment. Infinies variations des projections de la lumière. Projections d'ombres aussi. Les murs avec leurs différentes textures sont des surfaces où les ombres deviennent graphiques.
L'architecture du couvent nous apprend à voir toutes ces subtilités de la lumière. Elle nous invite à ne jamais être blasés par notre environnement. Elle préserve notre capacité d'émerveillement aux jeux d'ombre et de lumière : lumière ténue dans la quasi obscurité ; lumière délicate dans un escalier ; lumière canalisée par les ouvertures dans l'église ; lumière filtrée par les pans de verres ondulatoires de Iannis Xenakis.
Nous sommes ainsi provoqués, au quotidien, à saisir et goûter la délicatesse des jeux subtils, changeants et éphémères de la lumière. Ainsi, notre regard sur le couvent se renouvelle sans cesse, faisant de chaque déplacement, de chaque déambulation, une promenade architecturale où les surprises ne sont pas rares.
L'architecture du couvent invite à rester en éveil. Elle dispose à se laisser toucher par la poésie d'une lumière qui façonne jour après jour le regard, l'esprit et le cœur. Elle rend disponible à la poésie de l'impalpable et à la beauté de la vie. Elle nous prépare, frères dominicains, à la rencontre avec les hommes de notre temps et nous rend capables de percevoir en eux la lumière d'une vie intérieure. Pleinement incarnée, la lumière devient chemin de rencontre et d'élévation spirituelle.

Frère Marc Chauveau

Light at La Tourette

To live at the Dominican priory of Sainte-Marie de La Tourette is to inhabit a place of spirituality, built near Lyon by Le Corbusier in the late 1950s and now the setting for the communal life of some ten friars.
For Le Corbusier architecture was the fitting, skillful interplay between volumes assembled under light. He liked telling the friars that he had built the priory church out of two materials: concrete and light. The latter was a core element of his approach; he foregrounded it, focusing on the way it penetrates volumes.
We respond here to his formal meticulousness, to the effect on us of harmony of volume and balance of proportion. Le Corbusier speaks to us of inexpressible space. No ornamentation, no visual distractions, nothing superfluous. An economy of means that takes us straight to the essence of things, that teaches us to see and to contemplate—especially the play of light and shade on walls. Walls and floors transformed by shifting light. Infinite variations on projections of light. Projections of shadows as well. Shadows given a graphic quality by the different textures of the walls' surfaces.
The priory's architecture teaches us all these subtleties of light, urging us never to become blasé about our living environment. It preserves our capacity for wonderment at the interplay of light and shade: tenuous light in near darkness; delicate light in a staircase; light channelled through the church windows; light filtered through Iannis Xenakis's undulating sheets of glass.
Thus we are stimulated every day to seize and savor the exquisite elusiveness of these fine-drawn, ephemeral interactions. Our view of the monastery is endlessly renewed, making every change of place, every stroll an exploration full of surprises.
The architecture of the monastery enjoins us to stay on the alert. It inspires receptiveness to a poetry of light which, day after day, shapes the eye, the mind, and the heart. It opens us up to the poetry of the impalpable and the beauty of life. It readies us, as Dominican friars, for encounters with the people of our time and enables us to see in them the light of an inner life. Utterly embodied, light becomes a path to human contact and spiritual elevation.

Brother Marc Chauveau

Das Licht von La Tourette

Im Kloster von La Tourette zu leben, das bedeutet, einen spirituellen Ort zu bewohnen, ein architektonisches Werk, das Le Corbusier Ende der Fünfzigerjahre für die Dominikaner im Umland von Lyon geschaffen hat. Es ist heute Hort des religiösen Lebens einer Gemeinschaft von einem Dutzend Ordensbrüder.

Für Le Corbusier ist Architektur das richtige und gelehrte Zusammenspiel von unter Licht versammelten Volumina. Den Brüdern erzählte er gern, er habe die Klosterkirche mit zwei Materialien erbaut: mit Beton und Licht. Licht ist ein zentrales Element in der Architektur von Le Corbusier, der es inszeniert und der untersucht, wie es die Volumina durchdringt.

Wir sind berührt von der Strenge der architektonischen Formen. Die Harmonie der Volumina und das Gleichgewicht der Proportionen wirken auf uns ein. Le Corbusier spricht von einem *espace indicible*, einem unbeschreibbaren Raum. Keine Dekoration, keine visuelle Ablenkung, nichts Überflüssiges. Durch Reduktion werden wir zum Wesentlichen geführt. Das lehrt uns zu sehen, zu betrachten, insbesondere die Spiele von Schatten und Licht auf den Wänden. Unter dem sich verändernden Licht transformieren sich Wände und Böden. Unendliche Variationen von Lichtprojektionen. Und auch Schattenprojektionen. Die Mauern mit ihren unterschiedlichen Texturen gleichen lebendigen Oberflächen, auf denen die Schatten zu geometrischen und grafischen Zeichnungen werden.

Die Architektur des Klosters lehrt uns, all diese Feinheiten des Lichts wahrzunehmen. Sie legt uns nahe, uns niemals von unserer Umwelt überwältigen zu lassen. Sie bewahrt unsere Fähigkeit, angesichts dieser Spiele aus Schatten und Licht zu staunen: Licht in fast völliger Dunkelheit gehalten; delikates Licht in einem Treppenhaus; Licht, geleitet durch die Öffnungen in der Kirche; Licht, gefiltert durch die wellenförmigen Glasscheiben von Iannis Xenakis.

Wir werden derart immer wieder angeregt, die Feinheit der subtilen, sich wechselnden und flüchtigen Spiele des Lichts zu erfassen und zu genießen. So erneuert sich unser Blick auf das Kloster unablässig und macht jedes Sich-Fortbewegen, jedes Umherwandeln zu einem architektonischen Spaziergang, bei dem die Überraschungen nicht rar sind.

Die Architektur des Klosters lädt dazu ein, wach zu bleiben. Sie ist bereit, sich von der Poesie eines Lichts berühren zu lassen, das Tag für Tag den Blick, den Geist und das Herz bildet. Sie macht für die Poesie des Unfassbaren und die Schönheit des Lebens empfänglich. Sie bereitet uns dominikanische Ordensbrüder auf die Begegnung mit den Menschen unserer Zeit vor und befähigt uns, in ihnen das Licht eines inneren Lebens wahrzunehmen. Voll und ganz aufgenommen, wird das Licht zum Weg der Begegnung und der geistigen Aufrichtung.

Bruder Marc Chauveau

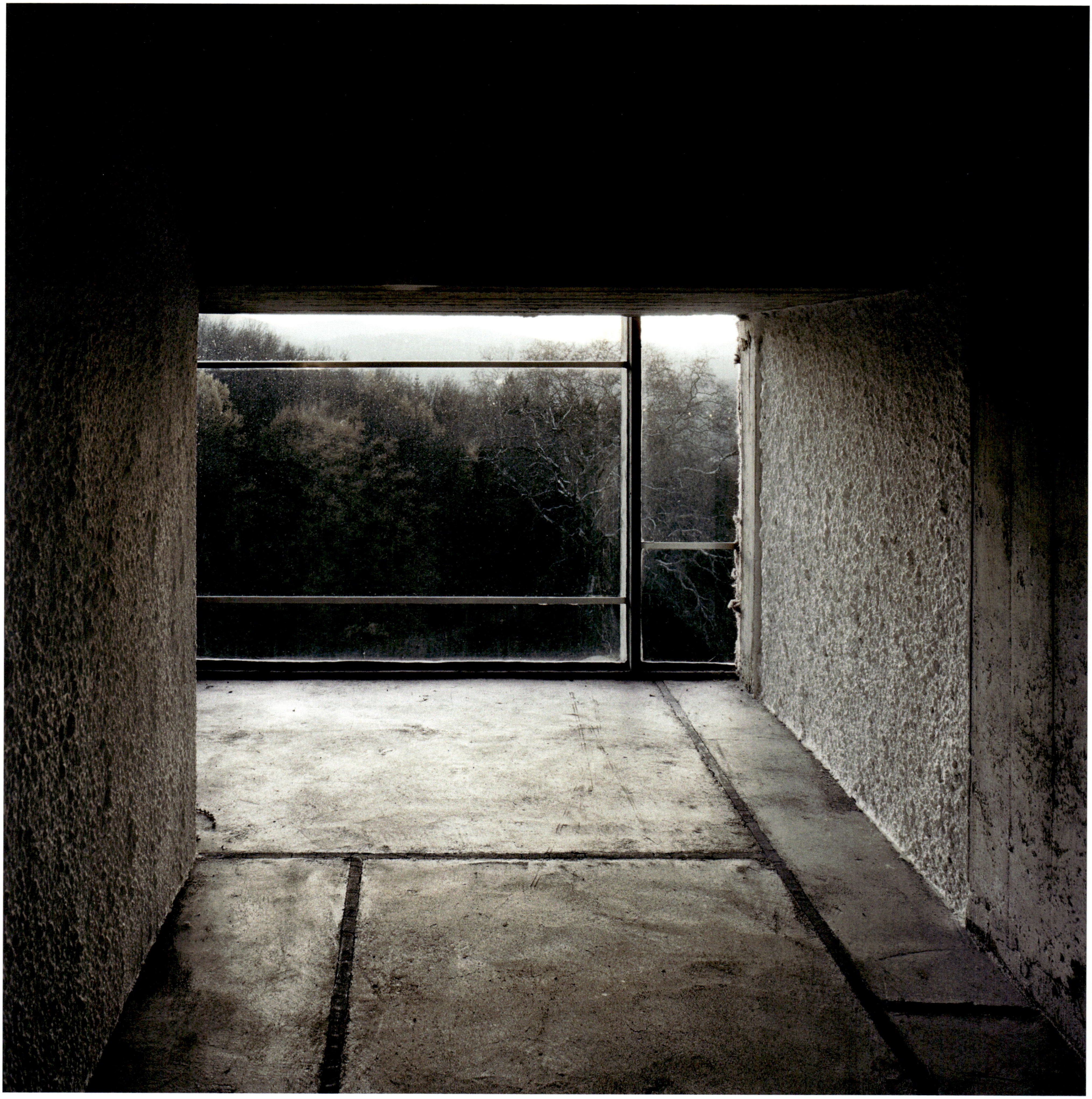

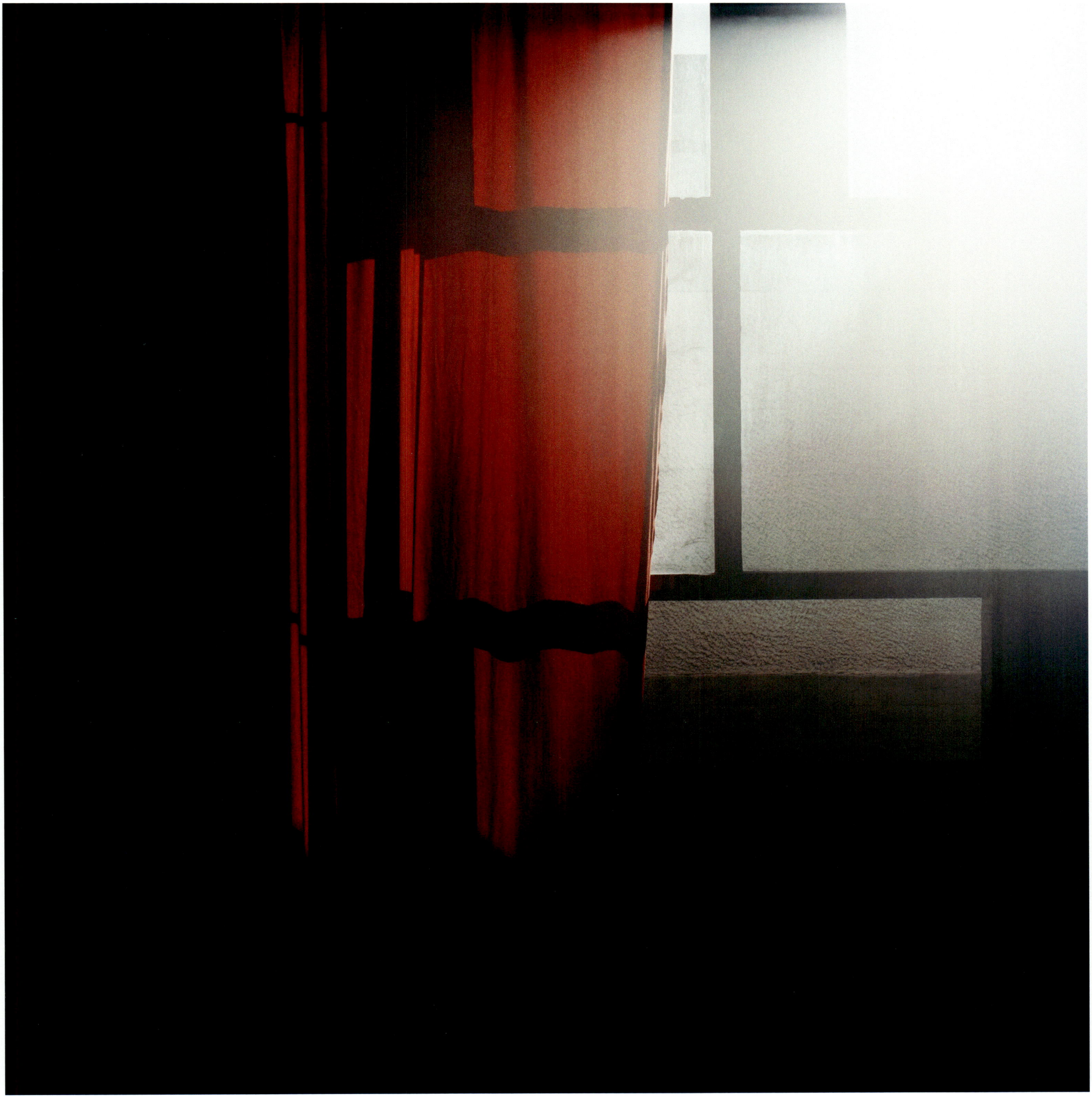

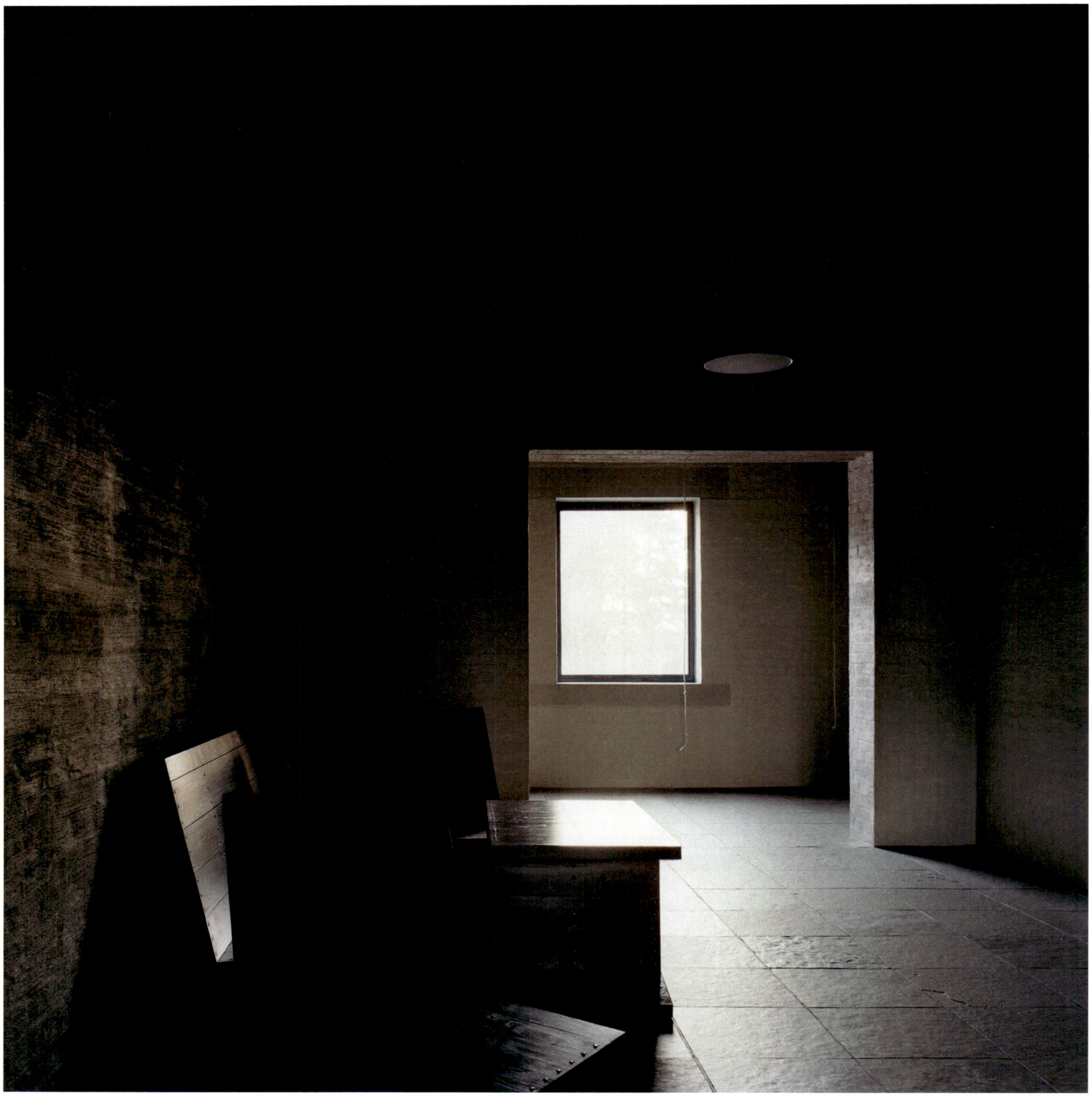

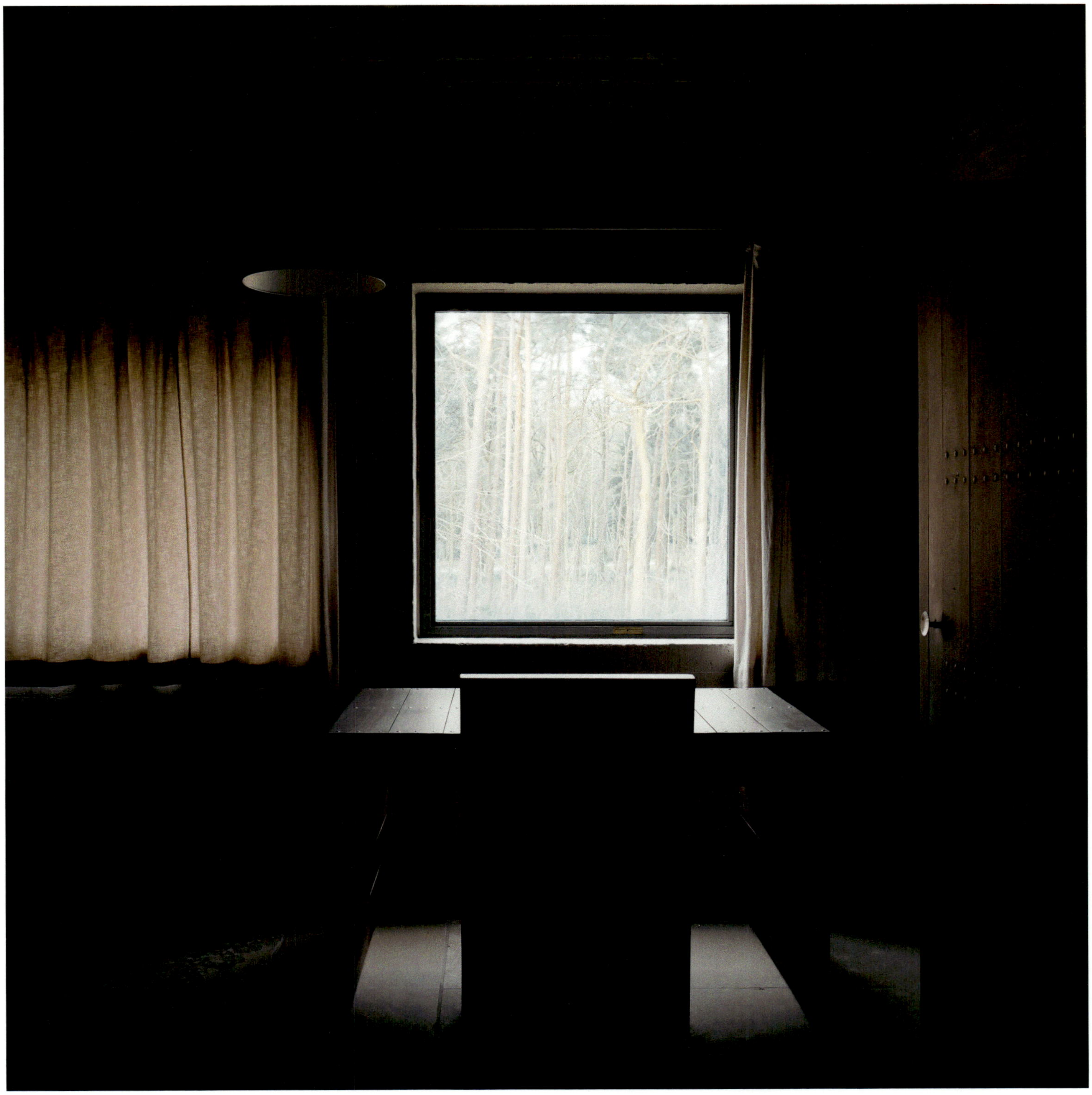

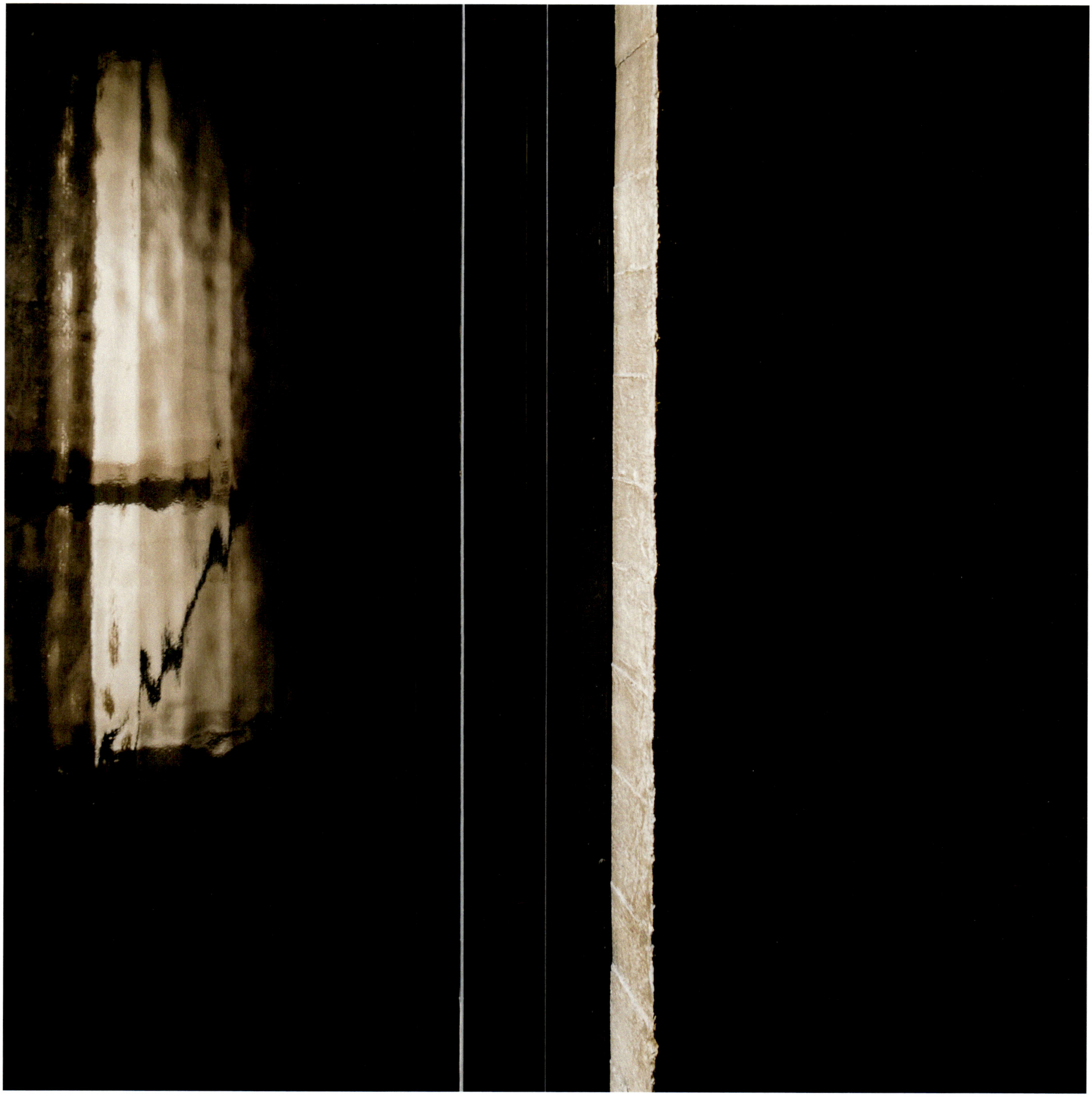

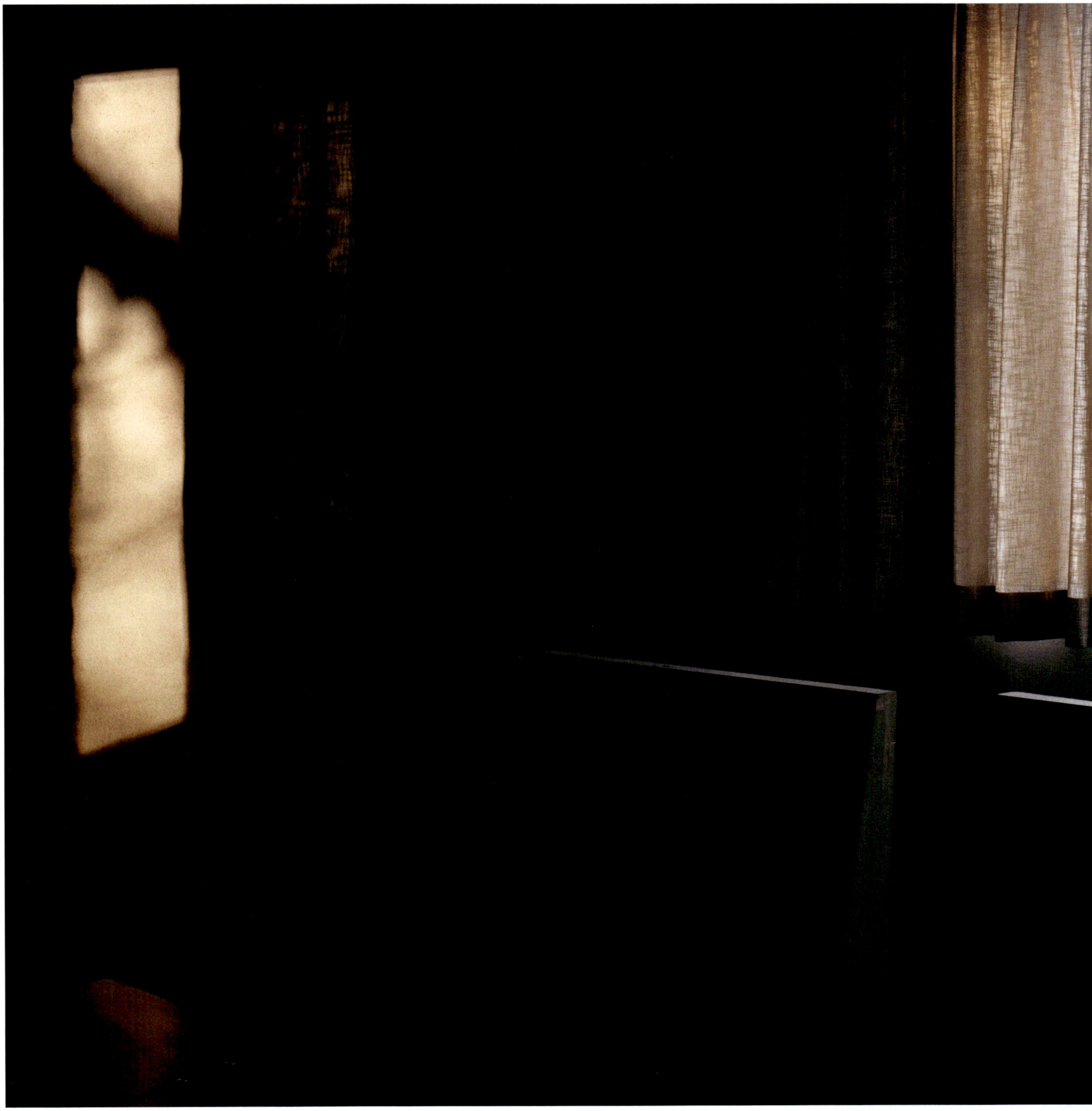

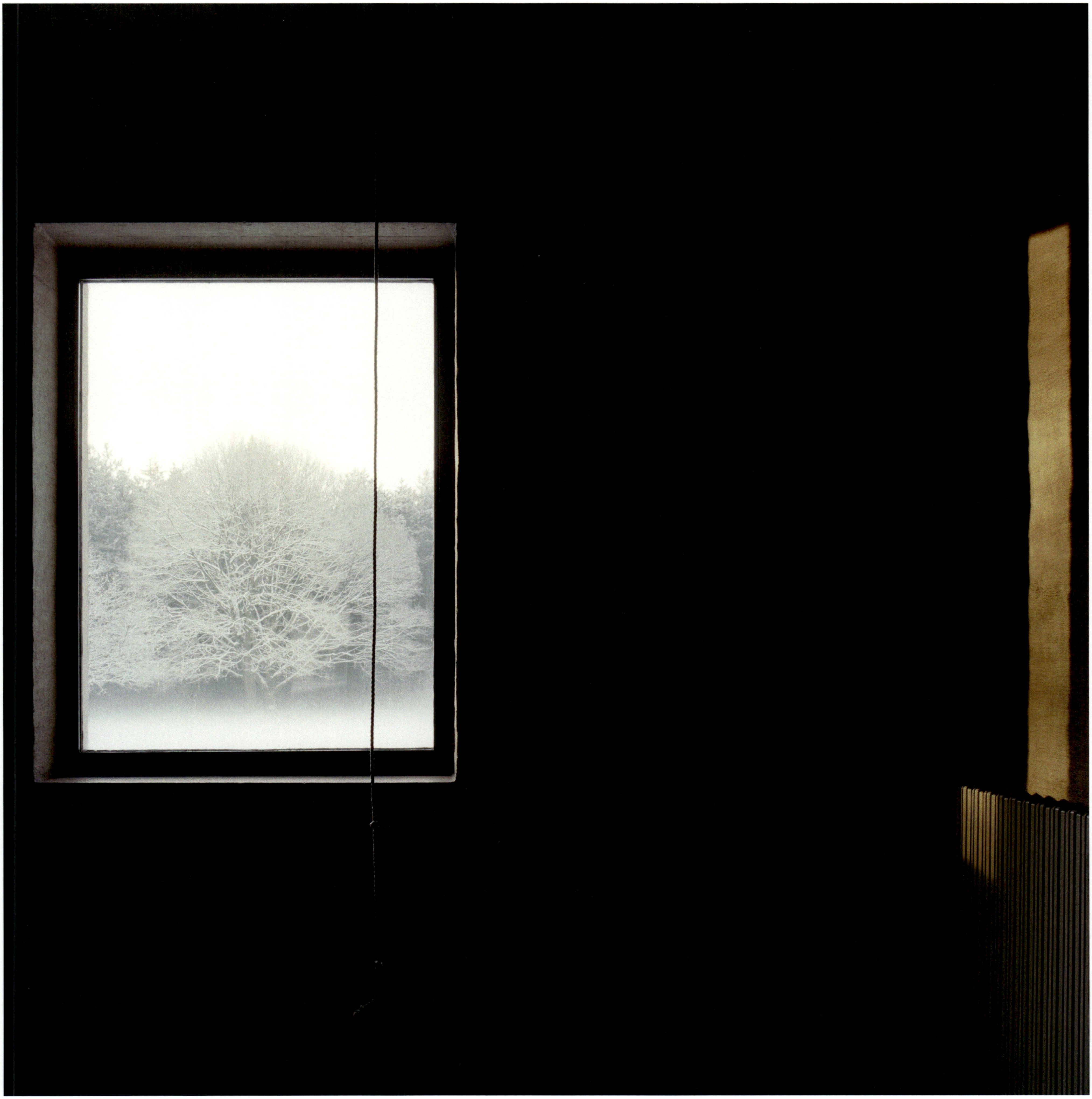

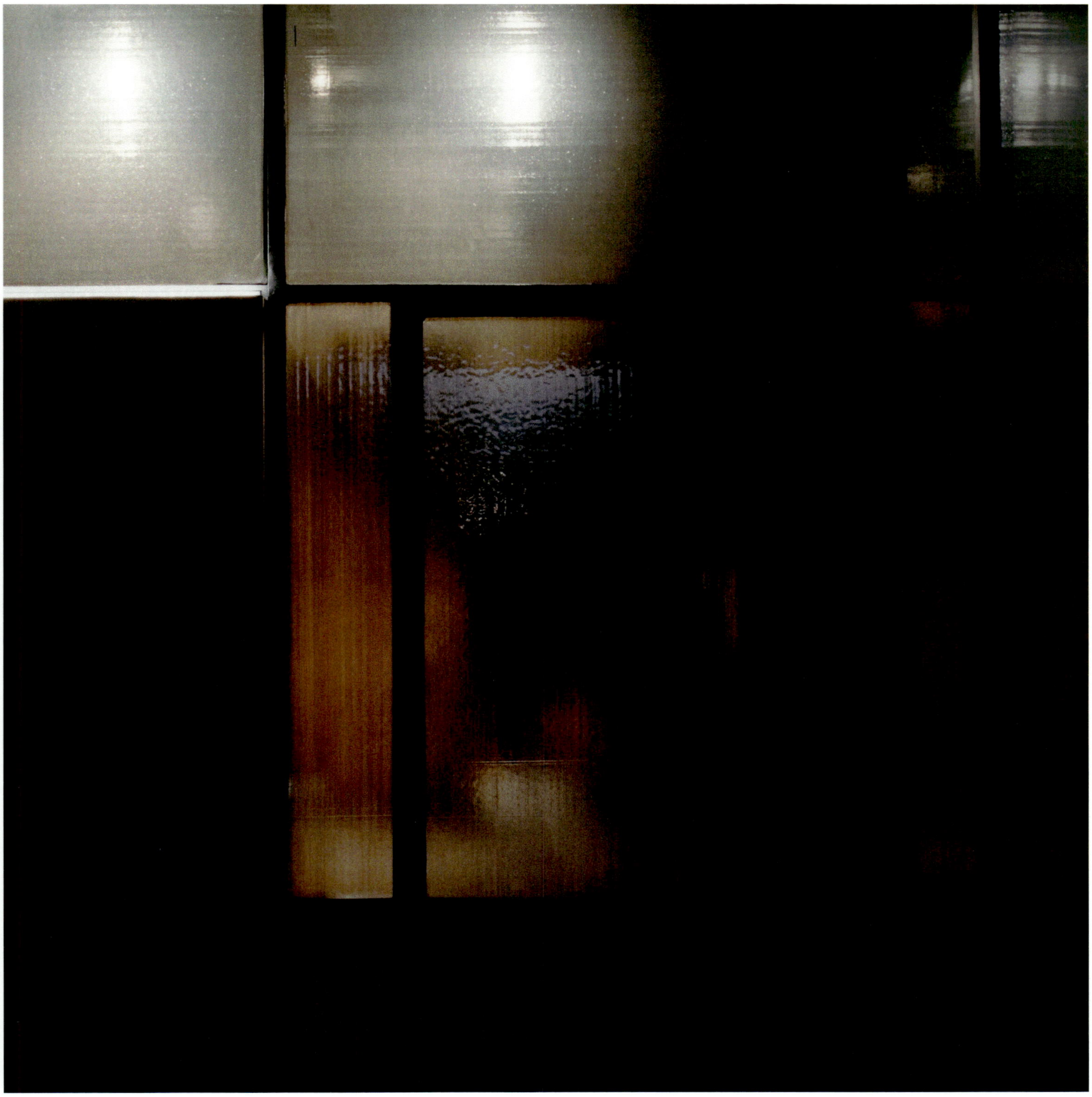

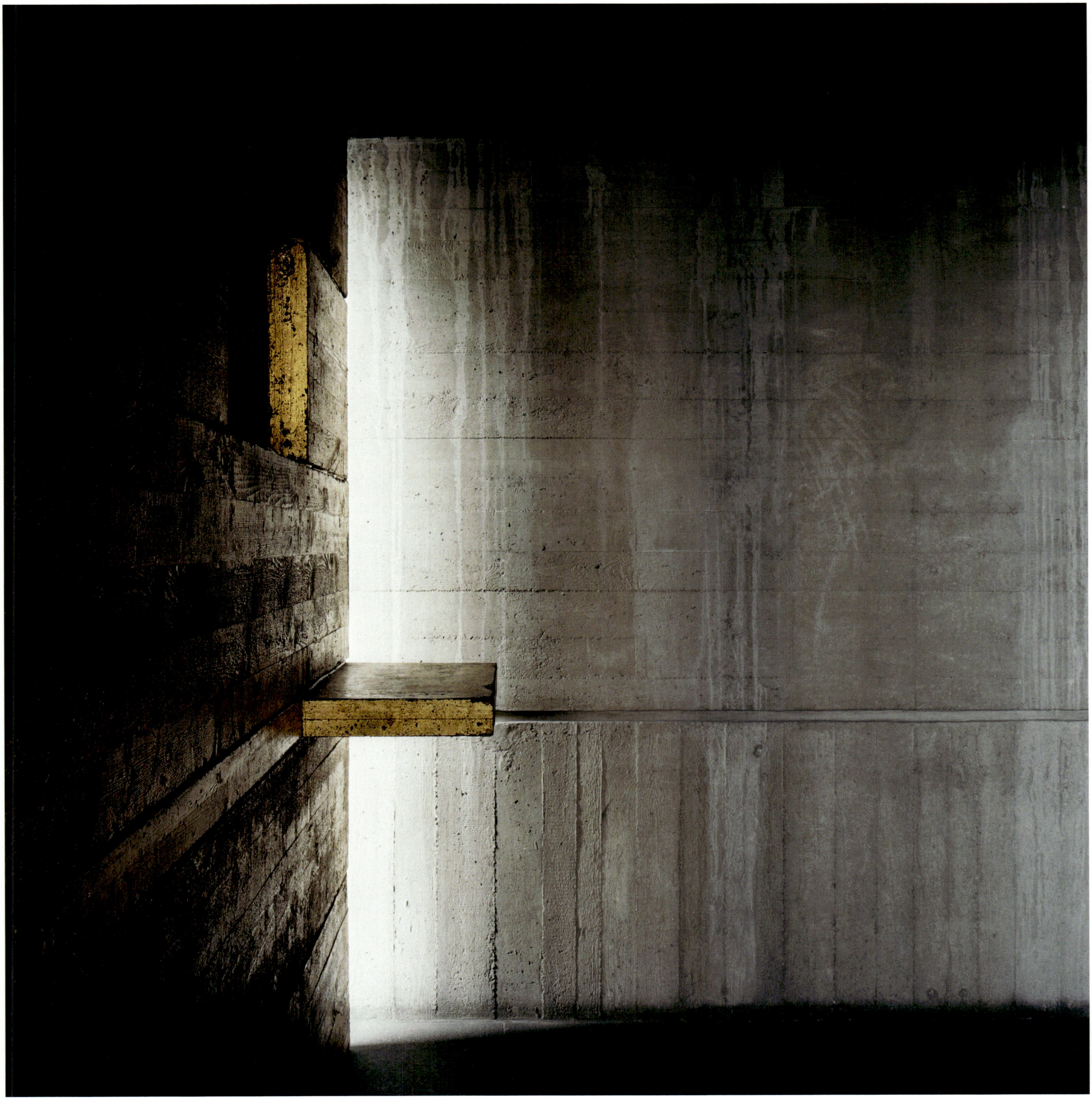

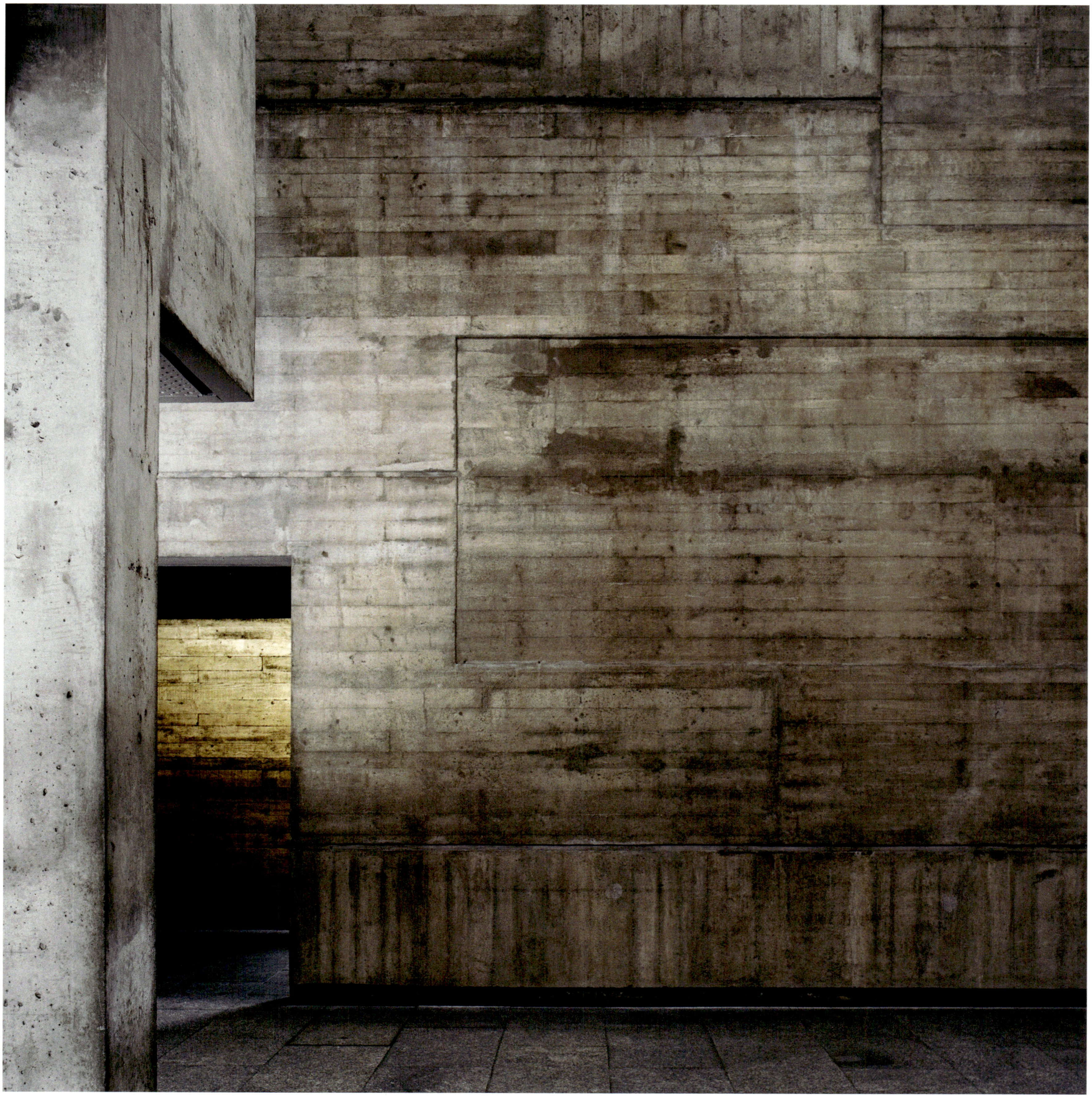

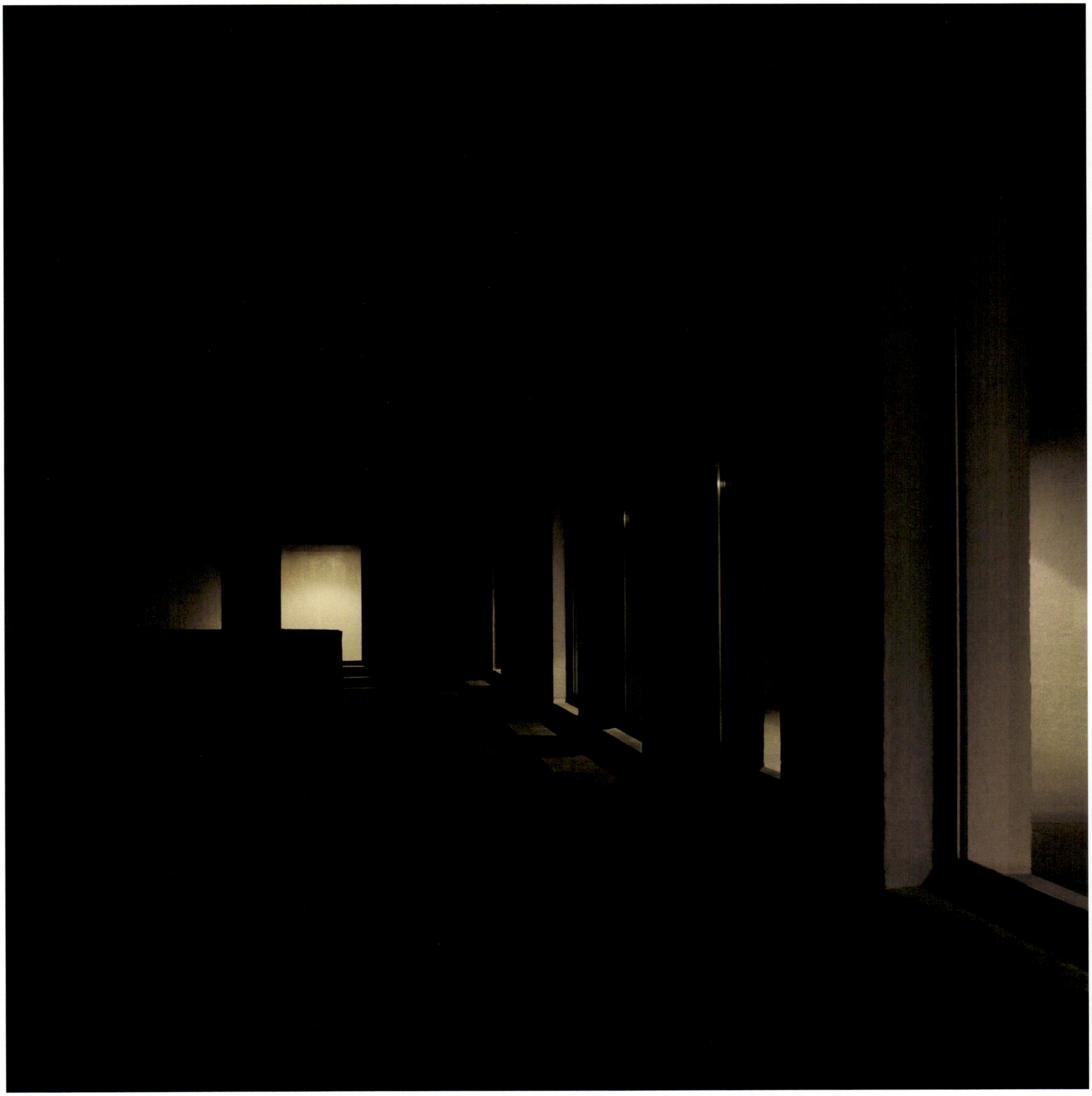

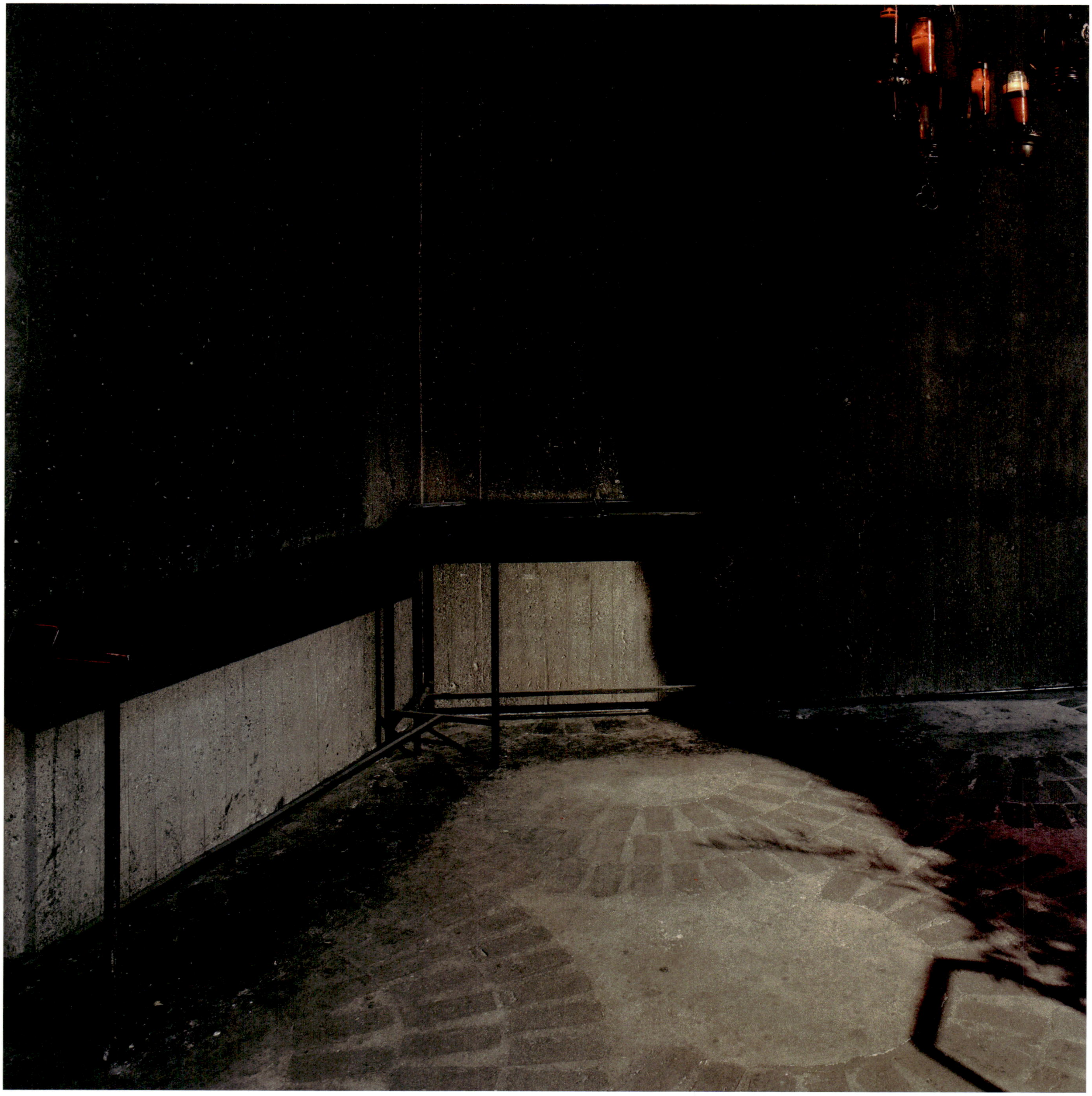

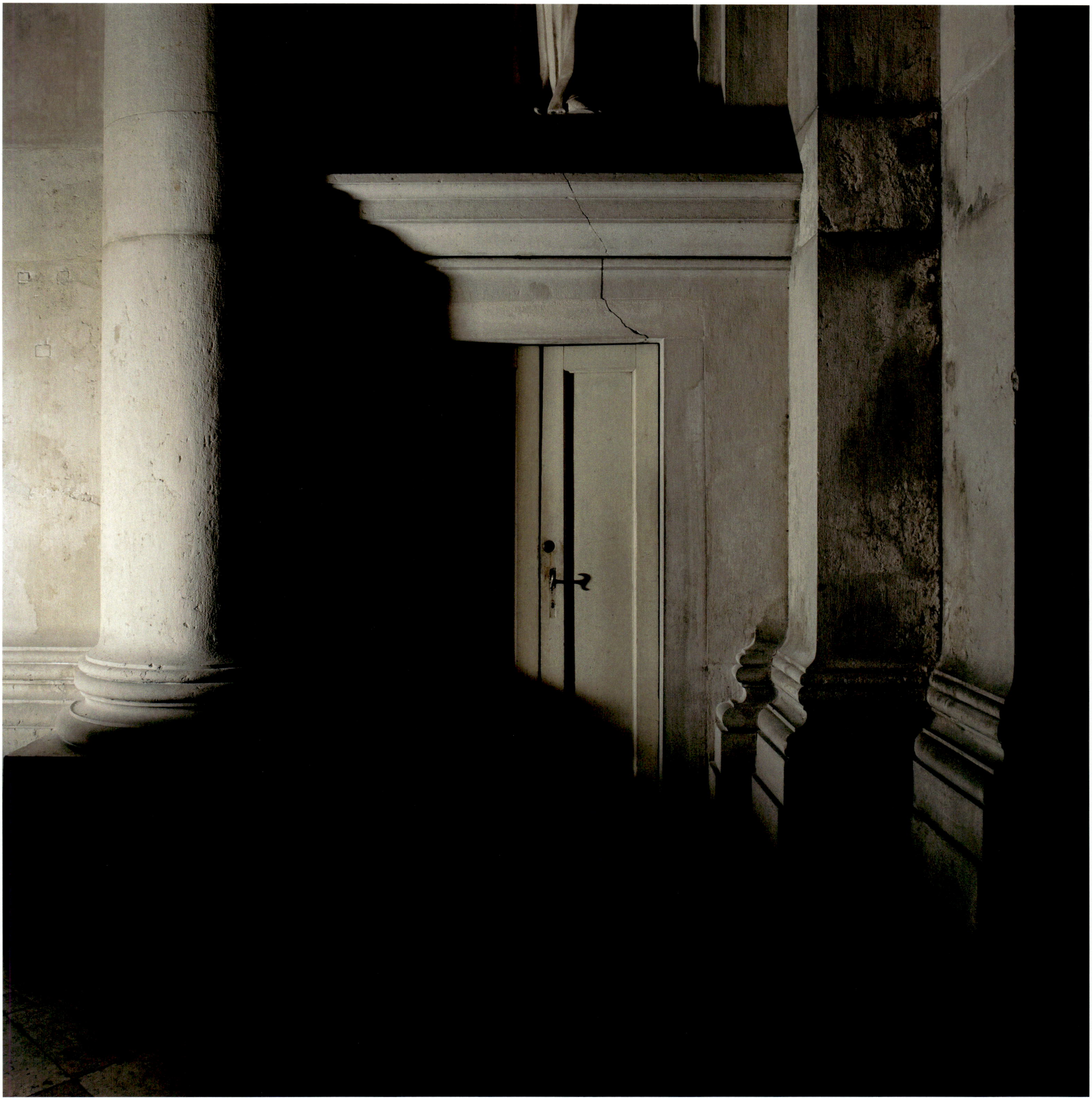

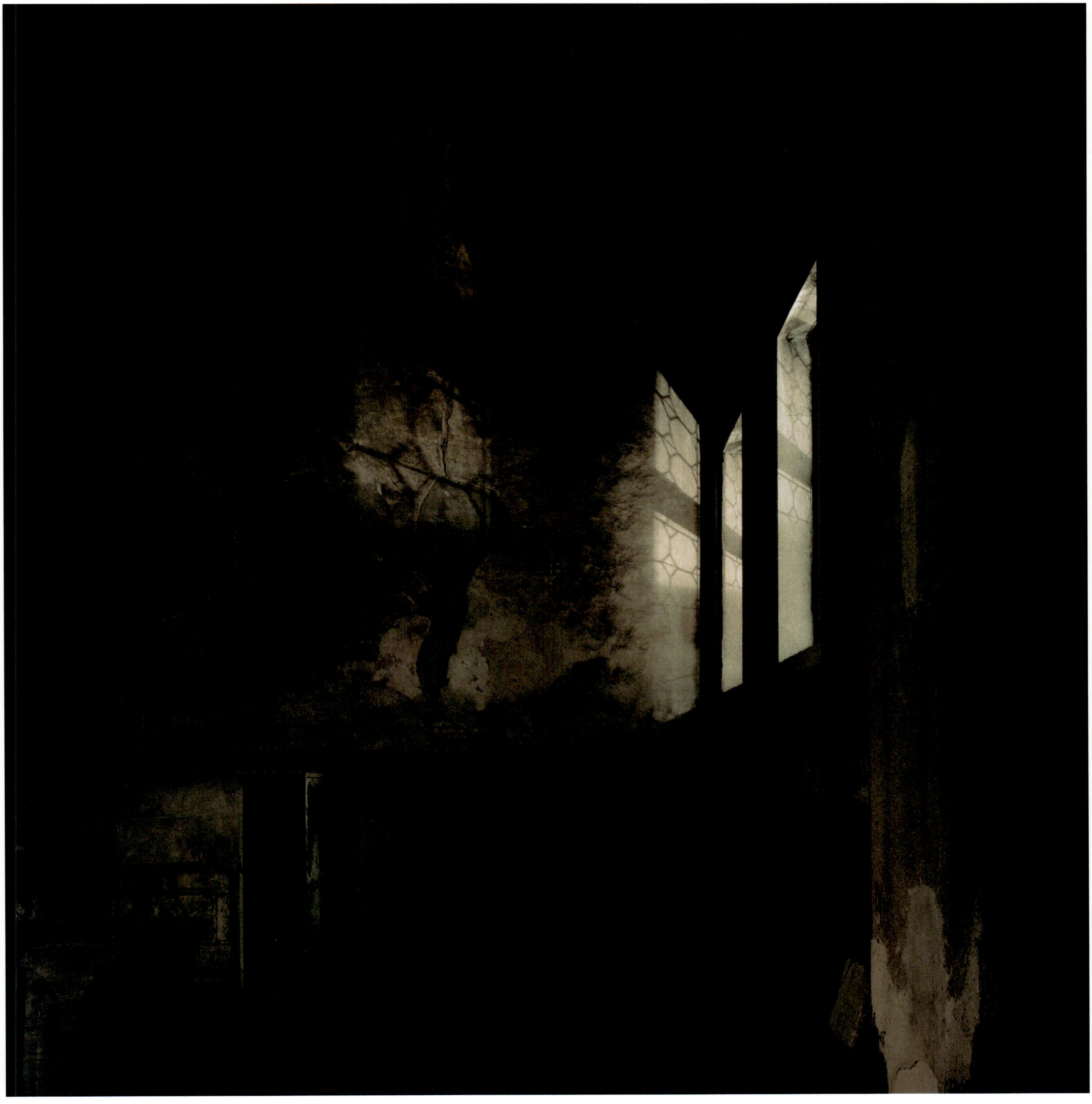

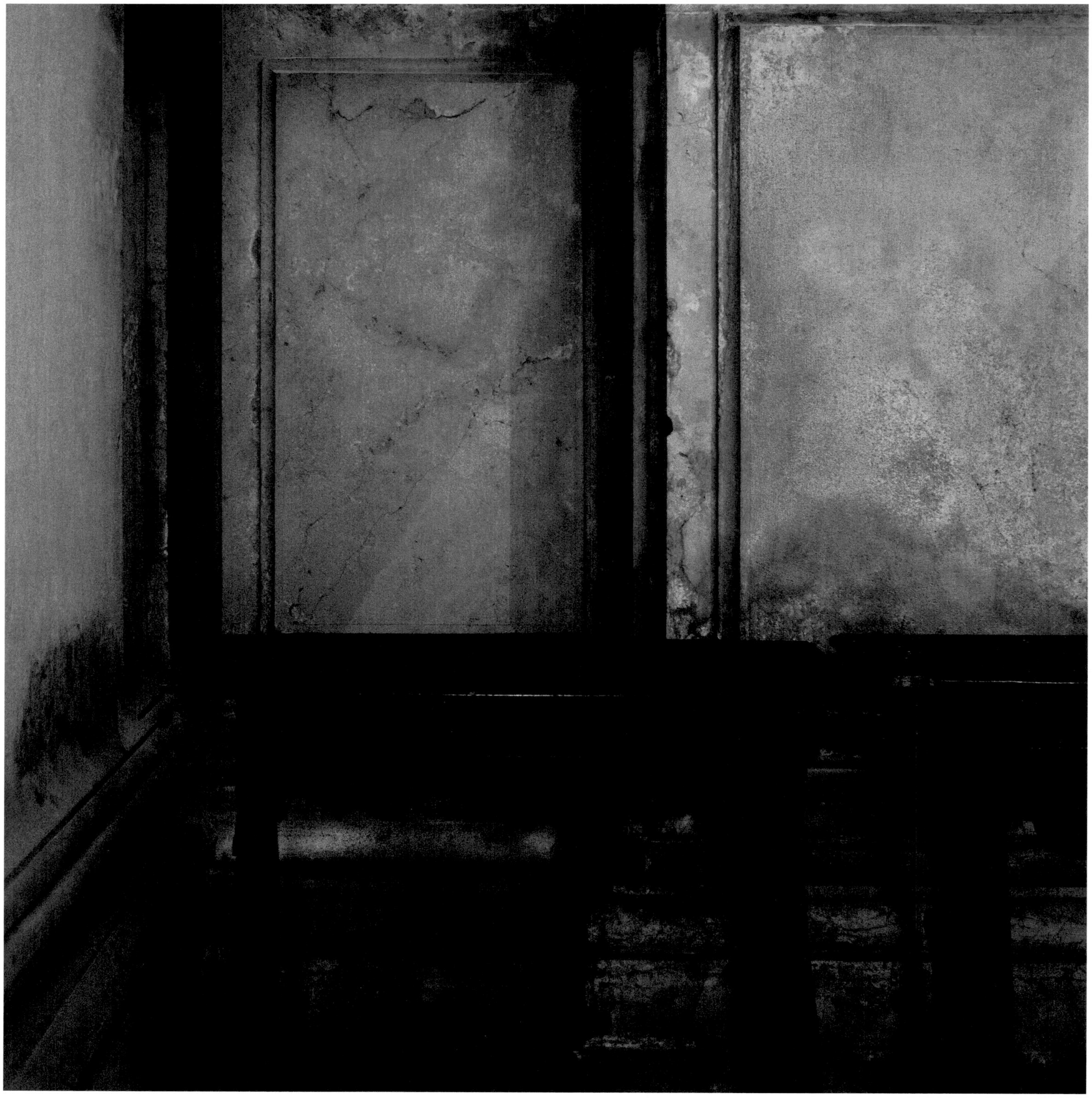

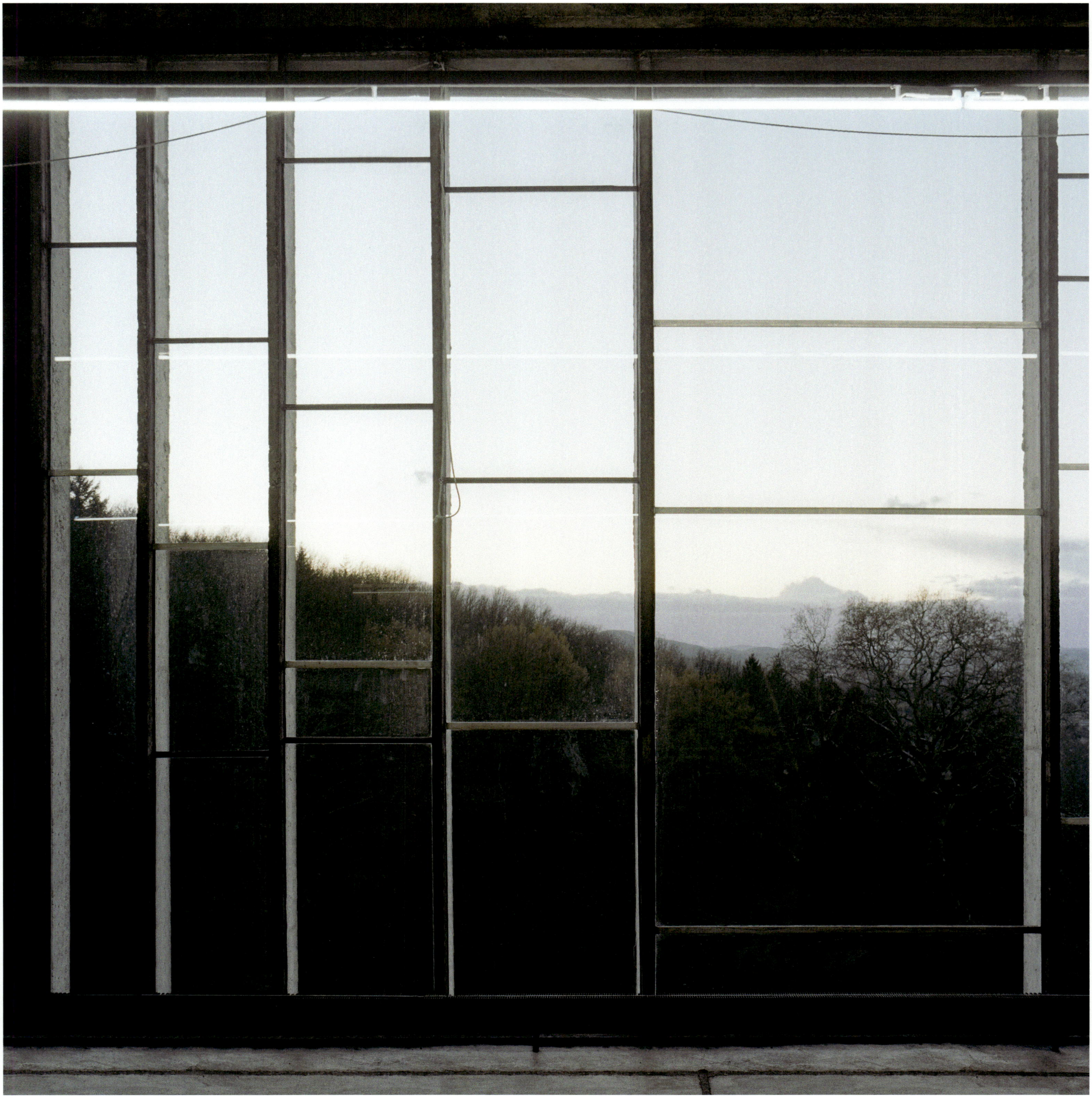

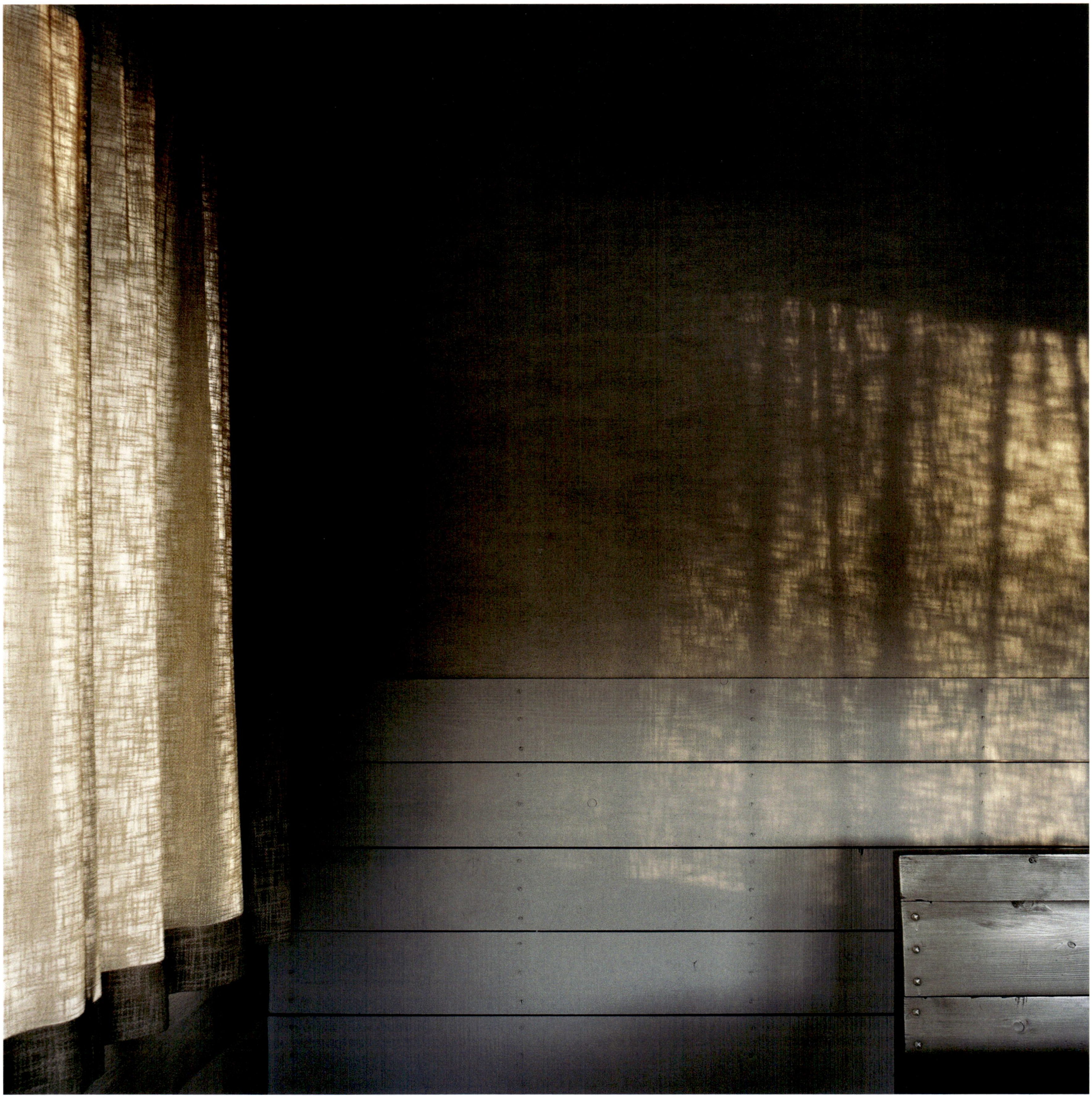

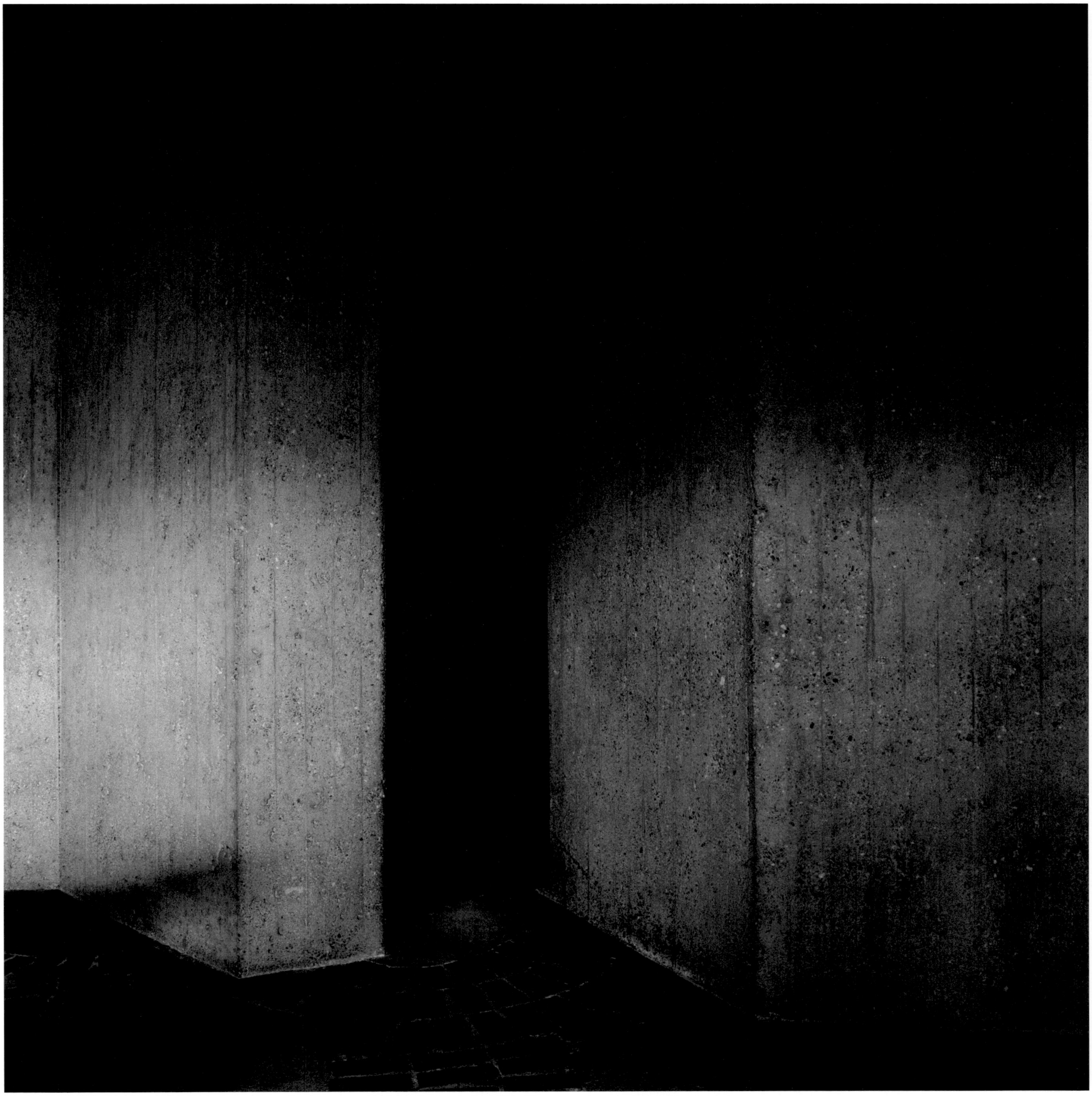

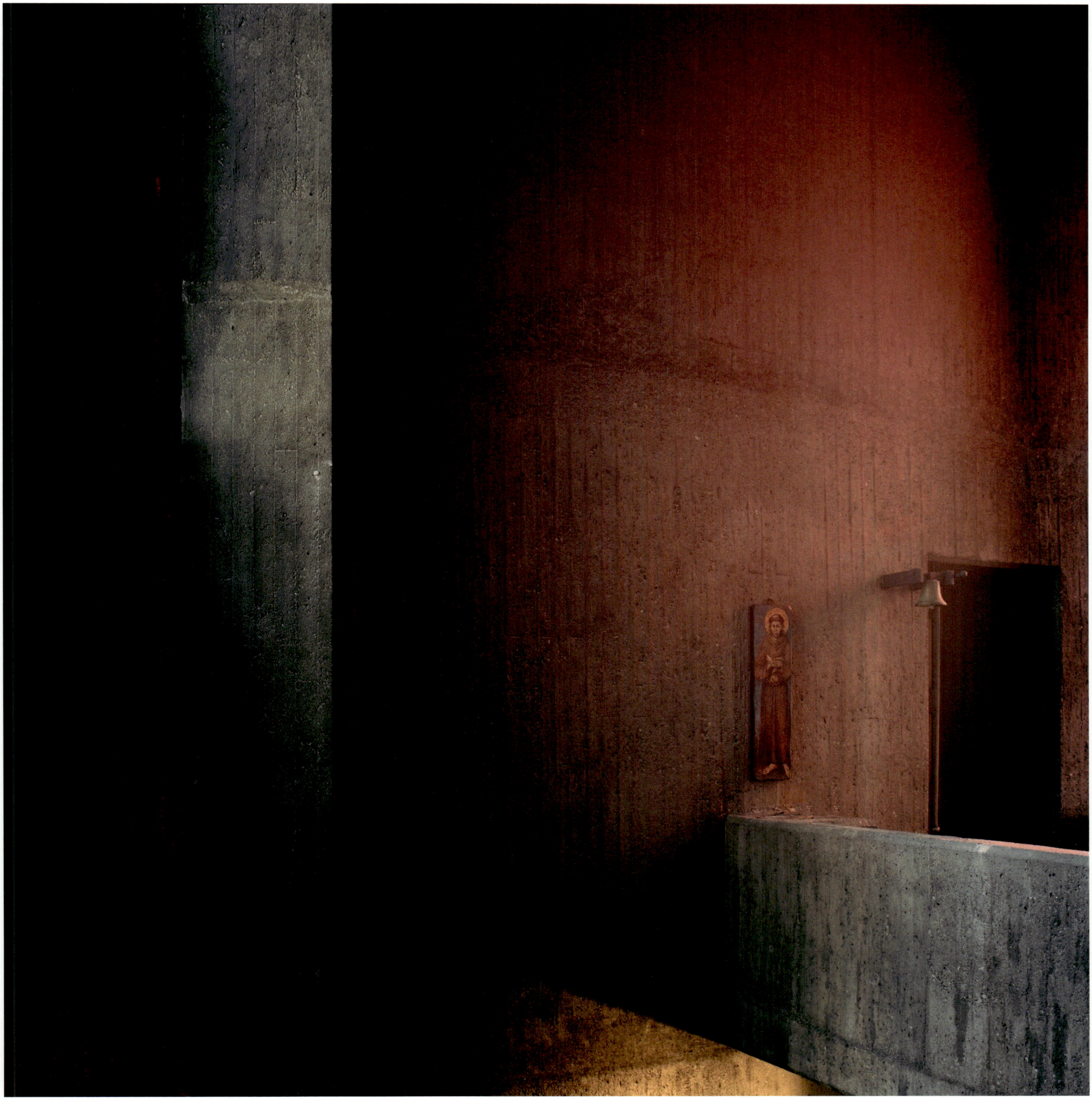

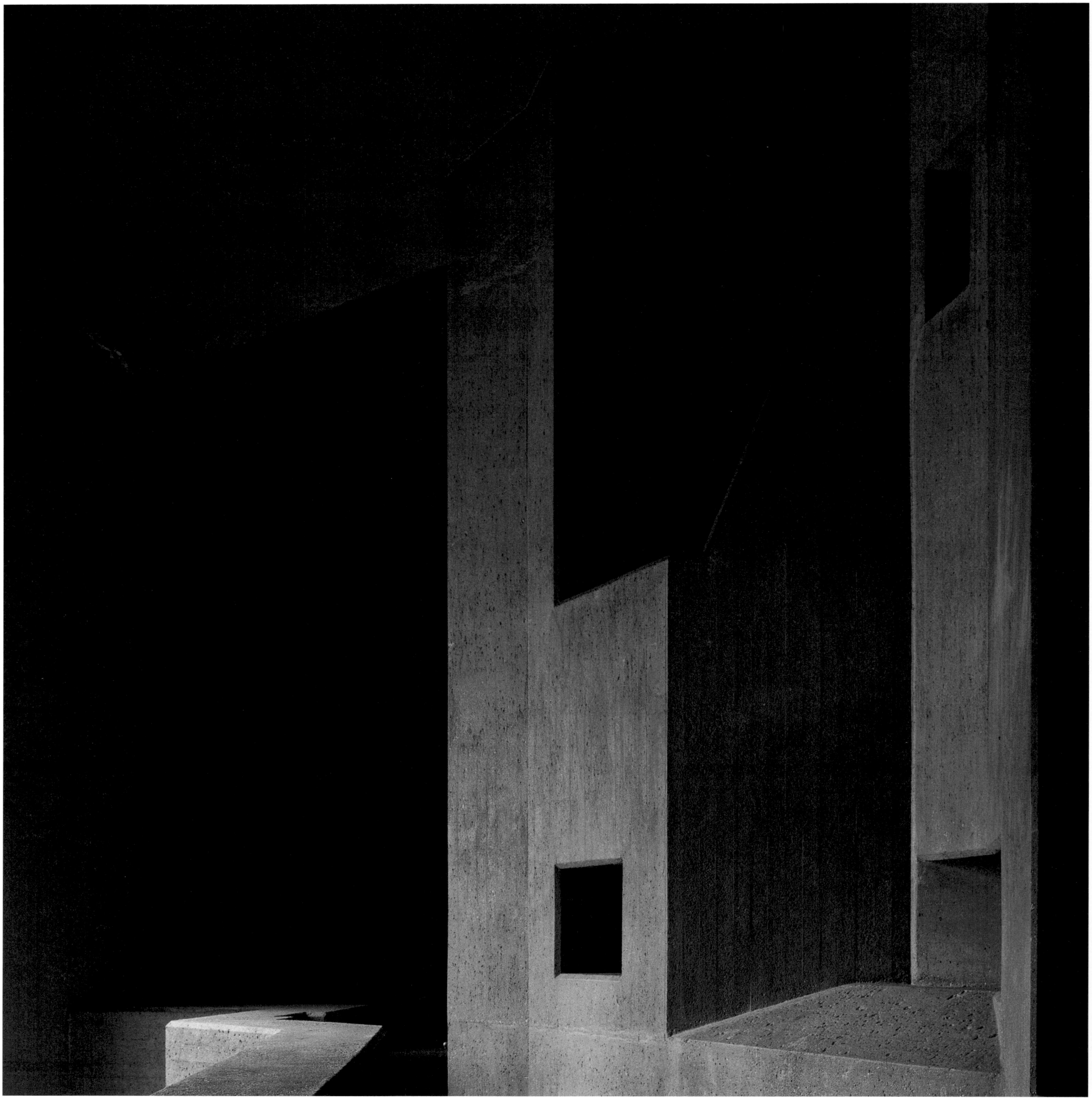

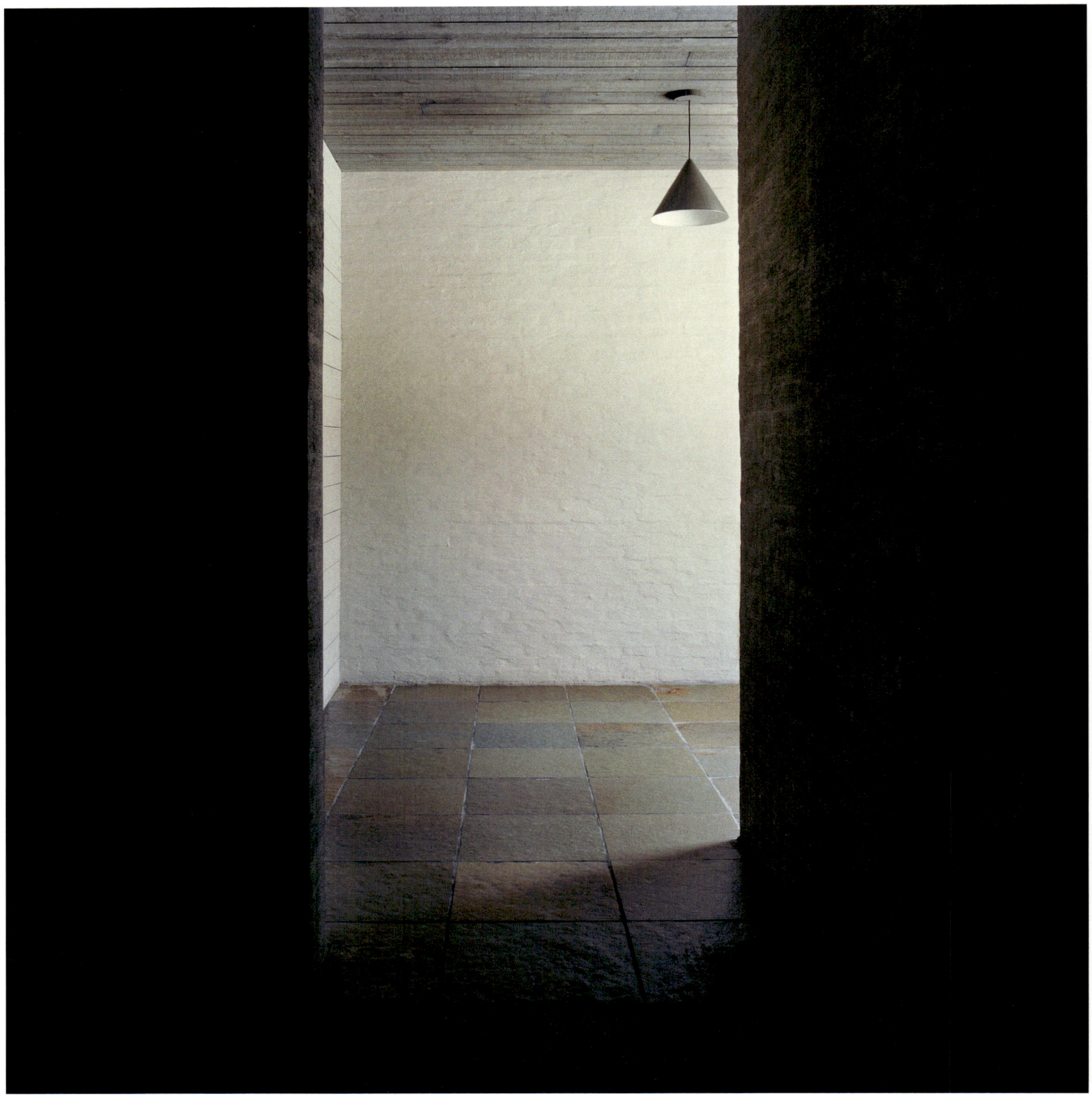

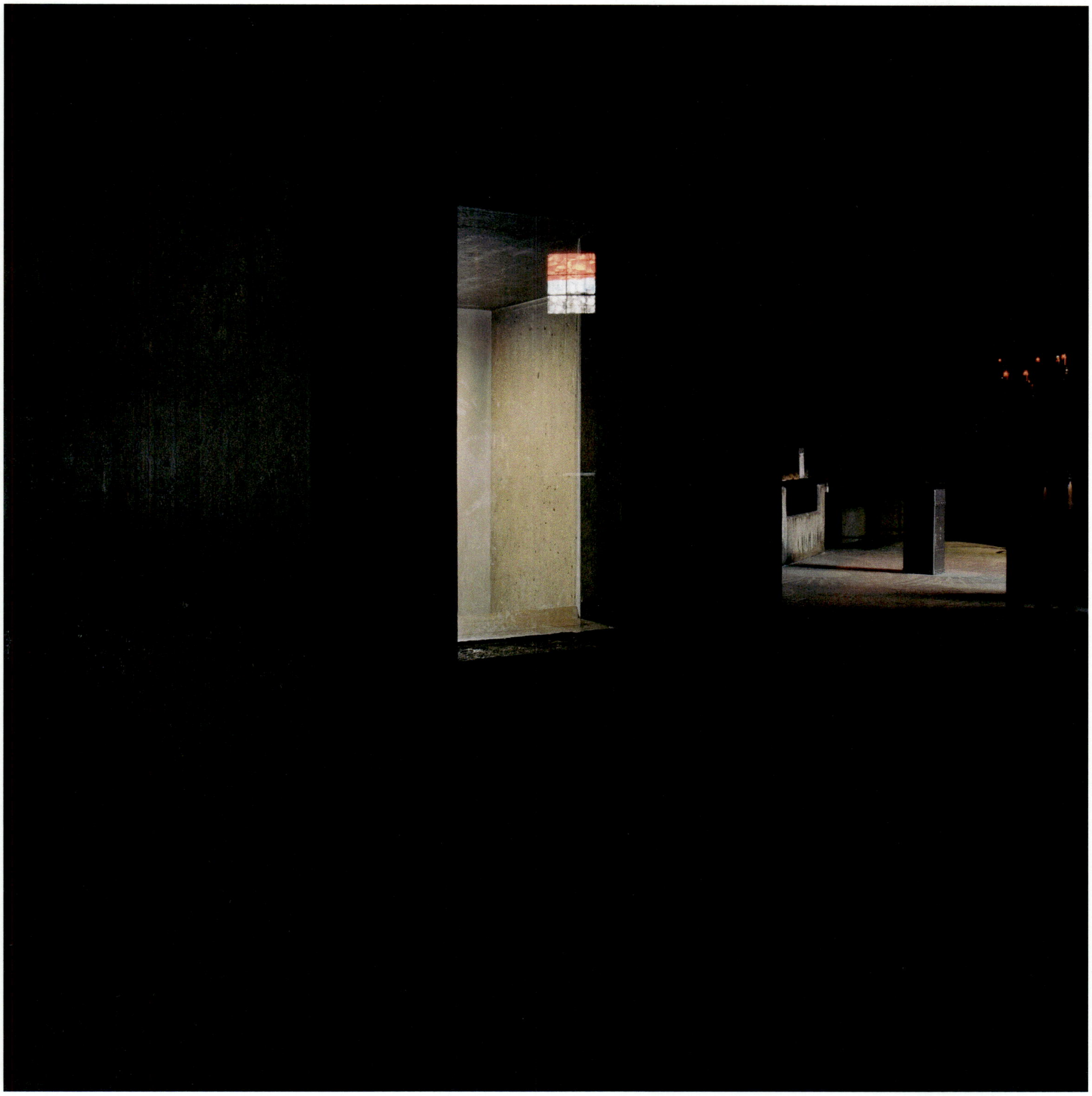

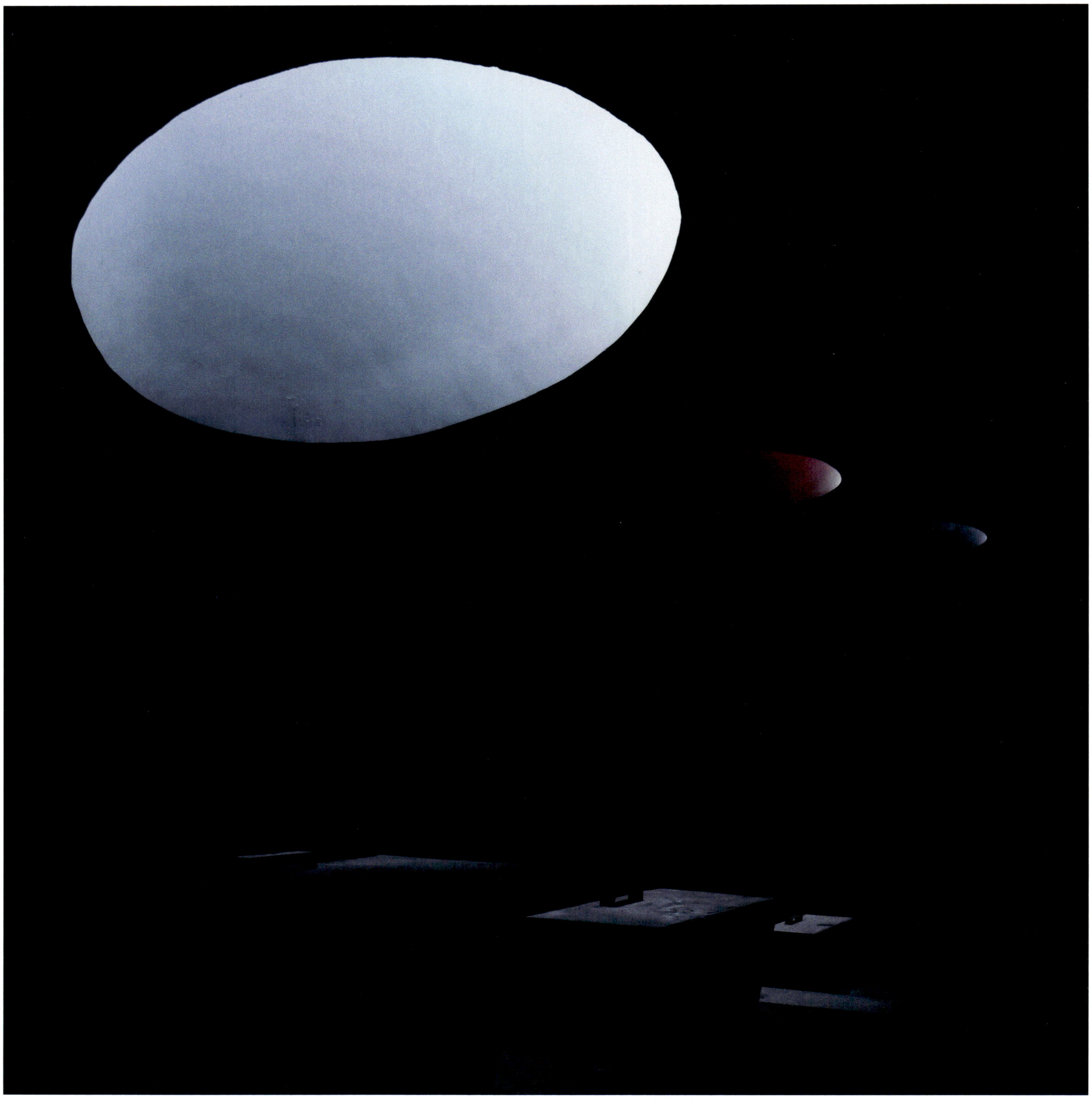

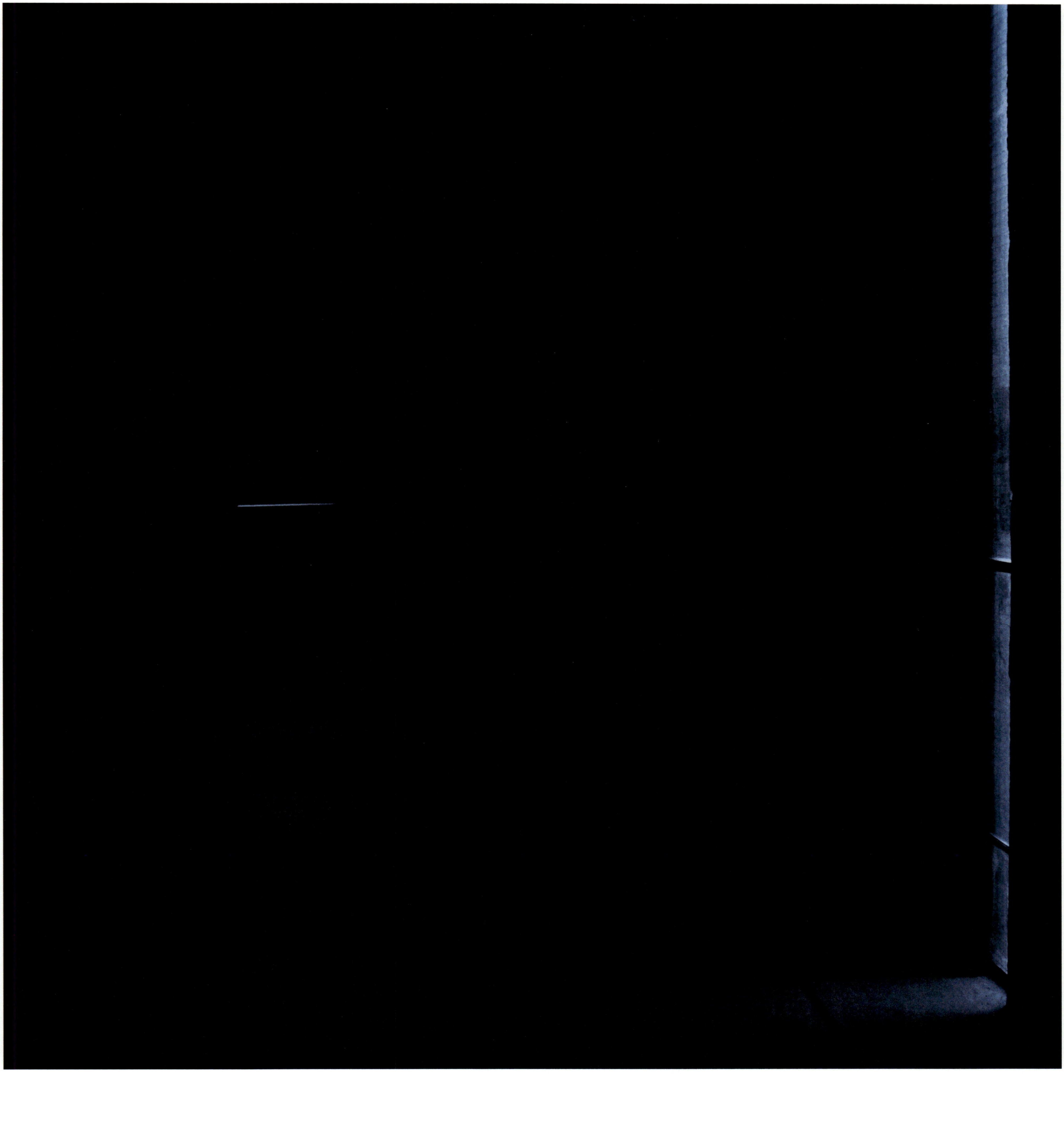

Monastery of Sainte-Marie de La Tourette
South of Lyon, France
Dominican Order ♂
Built 1956–60
Architect Charles-Édouard Jeanneret, known as Le Corbusier (1887–1965)
Visited March 2014
Page 14 Tourette 2
Page 17 Tourette 3
Page 52 Tourette 12
Page 55 Tourette 13
Page 59 Tourette 14
Page 62 Tourette 15
Page 39 Tourette 16

The building, nestled in the Beaujolais countryside, was originally designed as a Dominican school. Today only a few friars live and work here. Le Corbusier himself visited the site twice: once to inspect the grounds and once for the monastery's inauguration. After his death he returned a third time when, on the way to Paris, his body was laid out for a night in La Tourette. The massive complex, a structure of *béton brut* (unfinished concrete) that is set into the sloping topography on piers, is surrounded by woods and meadows. It contains one hundred cells based on the proportions of the Modulor system; each has a table, a bed, a chair, a sink behind the cupboard, and a window with a small balcony. The common areas, meanwhile, are spacious, with exceptional views of the surrounding landscape through meter-long glass façades. The crypt, with its many altars, was a very special experience for me. Here, the full moon surprised me with its strangely cool, focused light falling onto Le Corbusier's *canon de lumière* (light cannon).

Roosenberg Abbey
Waasmunster, Belgium
Franciscan Order ♀
Built 1972–74
Architect Dom Hans van der Laan (1904–1991)
Visited March 2015, February 2017
Page 29 Roosenberg 1
Page 46 Roosenberg 2
Page 40 Roosenberg 5
Page 18 Roosenberg 7
Page 23 Roosenberg 10
Page 19 Roosenberg 15
Page 21 Roosenberg 16
Page 48 Roosenberg

Not far from Ghent and Antwerp, this wonderful convent was commissioned by the Marian Sisters of the Franciscan order in the middle of a small park and designed by the architect and Benedictine monk Hans van der Laan. The choice of colors and materials is noteworthy: flagstones, whitewashed walls, and wood. Van der Laan also designed the furniture, creating a unified whole. Whenever I return to this place, I am amazed by the tranquility created by the architectural composition. It is an arrangement that has a direct correspondence with my work. The quite elderly sisters enter their church five times a day to sing and pray. I could hear their angelic voices through the corridors. Decades ago they recorded their truly ravishing singing, sensing that their voices would one day crack. They now live in a home for elderly sisters and still sing along to their tape recorder.

Memorial Church and Convent of Maria Regina Martyrum
Berlin, Germany
Carmelite Order ♀
Built 1960–63, 1982–84
Architects Hans Schädel (1910–1996) and Friedrich Ebert (1913–2002)
Visited November 2015
Page 42 Maria RM 1
Page 20 Maria RM 2
Page 51 Maria RM 3
Page 27 Maria RM 6
Page 25 Maria RM 7
Page 24 Maria RM 8
Page 56 Maria RM 9
Page 13 Maria RM 10
Page 28 Maria RM 11

Dedicated to the Christians who lost their lives in the resistance to National Socialism, the memorial church is located in the immediate vicinity of the execution site at Plötzensee. Bright and almost floating, it contrasts with the spacious memorial, a place that makes one feel rather uncomfortable. The church's interior is in accordance with the particularly beautiful lighting. The concrete walls are partly gilded, and the huge abstract altarpiece by Georg Meistermann represents the Revelation. The convent itself is located on the neighboring property. It was a particularly interesting experience for me to live in a convent in my own city for a while. The wonderful nuns made it easy for me because, although they live there in seclusion from the world, they are open-minded and interested in everything that happens in this city.

Monastery of San Giorgio Maggiore
Venice, Italy
Benedictine Order ♂
Built 1565–1610
Architect Andrea Palladio (1508–1580)
Visited January 2018
Page 31 SGM 2
Page 33 SGM 7
Page 35 SGM 11
Page 36 SGM 8

I have had the opportunity to live in the Palladian monastery on this Venetian island several times. From my balcony I can look across the water to the Piazza San Marco. It is an unforgettable view, especially in the early morning, when the city begins to glow in soft colors. Just a five-minute *vaporetto* ride from the hustle and bustle of Venice, I find peace and tranquility behind the thick walls of this three-aisled basilica. The sanctuary is crowned by an enormous dome, behind which are the choir stalls made of precious wood. Jacopo Tintoretto's paintings are dimly lit; their spatial concept makes me feel both sublime and small. Vittore Carpaccio's wonderful Saint George killing the dragon hangs in the monastery part of the complex.
Between my working hours, I look forward to lunch with the monks; they are excellent cooks, and we dine together in the refectory while listening to a reading. Behind the monastery they keep hens. The cockerel, as one might have guessed, is called Tintoretto.

Cathedral of St. Mary, Queen of Peace
Neviges, Germany
Franciscan Order ♂
Built 1966–68
Architect Gottfried Böhm (born 1920)
Visited January 2013
Page 30 Transept 13
Page 41 Transept 16
Page 44 KDF 1
Page 43 KDF 3
Page 47 KDF 4

The Cathedral of St. Mary towers over Neviges. Its shape is reminiscent of huge blocks of stone; it also makes me think of the Expressionist lines and surfaces of paintings by Lyonel Feininger. When you enter the building, it takes a while for your eyes to get used to the darkness. Gradually the church, designed by Gottfried Böhm, starts to resemble a sacred city of exposed concrete. The light penetrates the interior here and there, sometimes more intensely and sometimes less, through windows that were also designed by the architect. Their rich red outshines the gray of the concrete, which seems to glow ceremoniously when the sun is shining brightly. Time and again I notice young people lying down in front of the altar, saying prayers amid the Brutalism.

Kloster Sainte-Marie de La Tourette
Südlich von Lyon, Frankreich
Dominikanerorden ♂
Gebaut 1956–1960
Architekt Charles-Édouard Jeanneret, bekannt als Le Corbusier (1887–1965)
Aufenthalt März 2014
Seite 14 Tourette 2
Seite 17 Tourette 3
Seite 52 Tourette 12
Seite 55 Tourette 13
Seite 59 Tourette 14
Seite 62 Tourette 15
Seite 39 Tourette 16

Das in die Landschaft des Beaujolais eingebettete Gebäude wurde ursprünglich als dominikanische Lehrstätte gebaut. Heute bewohnen und bewirtschaften es wenige Ordensbrüder. Le Corbusier ist selbst nur zweimal hier gewesen. Einmal, um sich das Gelände anzusehen, einmal bei der Einweihung des Klosters. Erst nach seinem Tod kam es zu einem dritten Aufenthalt: Auf dem Weg nach Paris wurde er für eine Nacht in La Tourette aufgebahrt.
Der Komplex ist mächtig, ein *béton brut* auf Stützen in die abfallende Hangtopografie gestellt, von Wald und Wiesen umgeben. Er beherbergt hundert Zellen, nach Modulor-Maßen gebaut: Tisch, Bett, Stuhl, ein Waschbecken hinter dem Schrank, ein Fenster mit einem Austritt. Großzügig sind wiederum die Gemeinschaftsräume angelegt, mit bemerkenswerter Öffnung zur umliegenden Landschaft durch meterlange Glasfronten. Die Krypta mit ihren vielen Altären war ein ganz besonderes Erlebnis für mich. Hier überraschte mich der Vollmond mit einem seltsam kühlen, gebündelten Licht über Corbusiers *canon de lumière.*

Abtei Roosenberg
Waasmunster, Belgien
Franziskanerorden ♀
Gebaut 1972–1974
Architekt Dom Hans van der Laan (1904–1991)
Aufenthalt März 2015, Februar 2017
Seite 29 Roosenberg 1
Seite 46 Roosenberg 2
Seite 40 Roosenberg 5
Seite 18 Roosenberg 7
Seite 23 Roosenberg 10
Seite 19 Roosenberg 15
Seite 21 Roosenberg 16
Seite 48 Roosenberg

Unweit von Gent und Antwerpen haben sich die Marienschwestern vom Franziskanerorden dieses wunderbare Kloster inmitten eines kleinen Parks vom Architekten und Benediktinermönch Hans van der Laan bauen lassen. Es besticht durch seine Farb- und Materialwahl: Steinplatten, hell geschlemmte Wände, Holz. Und weil Hans van der Laan auch die Möbel entworfen hat, scheint alles wie aus einem Guss. Wann immer ich an diesen Ort zurückkehre, erstaunt mich die Ruhe, die von der architektonischen Komposition ausgeht. Eine Anordnung, die in mir eine unmittelbare Entsprechung findet.
Die sehr alten Schwestern gehen fünfmal täglich in ihre Kirche, um zu singen und zu beten. Durch die Gänge konnte ich ihre engelsgleichen Stimmen vernehmen. Schon vor Jahrzehnten zeichneten sie ihren wirklich hinreißenden Gesang auf, in der Vorausahnung, ihre Stimmen könnten im Alter brüchig werden. Inzwischen leben sie in einem Nonnen-Altersheim und singen nach wie vor zu ihrem Tonband.

Gedenkkirche und Kloster Maria Regina Martyrum
Berlin, Deutschland
Karmeliterorden ♀
Gebaut 1960–1963, 1982–1984
Architekt Hans Schädel (1910–1996) und Friedrich Ebert (1913–2002)
Aufenthalt November 2015
Seite 42 Maria RM 1
Seite 20 Maria RM 2
Seite 51 Maria RM 3
Seite 27 Maria RM 6
Seite 25 Maria RM 7
Seite 24 Maria RM 8
Seite 56 Maria RM 9
Seite 13 Maria RM 10
Seite 28 Maria RM 11

Gewidmet den Gläubigen, die im Widerstand gegen den Nationalsozialismus ihr Leben ließen, liegt die Gedenkkirche in unmittelbarer Nähe zur Hinrichtungsstätte Plötzensee. Hell, fast schwebend, hebt sie sich von der weiträumigen Erinnerungsstätte ab, einem Ort, der fast Unbehagen auslöst. Der Innenraum dieser Kirche stimmt mit der besonders schönen Lichtführung versöhnlich. Die Betonwände sind zum Teil vergoldet und das riesige abstrakte Altarbild von Georg Meistermann zeigt die Offenbarung. Das Kloster selbst befindet sich auf dem Nachbargrundstück.
In meiner eigenen Stadt eine Weile in einem Kloster zu wohnen, war eine besonders interessante Erfahrung. Die liebenswerten Nonnen machten es mir leicht, denn obwohl sie dort zurückgezogen leben, sind sie aufgeschlossen und interessiert an allem, was in dieser Stadt passiert.

Kloster San Giorgio Maggiore
Venedig, Italien
Benediktinerorden ♂
Gebaut 1565–1610
Architekt Andrea Palladio (1508–1580)
Aufenthalt Januar 2018
Seite 31 SGM 2
Seite 33 SGM 7
Seite 35 SGM 11
Seite 36 SGM 8

Gleich mehrfach durfte ich in dem Palladio-Kloster auf der Insel vor Venedig wohnen. Von meinem Balkon schaute ich über das Wasser auf die Piazza San Marco. Ein unvergesslicher Blick, besonders am frühen Morgen, wenn die Stadt in sanften Farben zu leuchten beginnt. Nur fünf Minuten mit dem *vaporetto* abseits des Trubels bin ich in Stille hinter den dicken Mauern der dreischiffigen Basilika. Der Altarraum wird von einer enormen Kuppel gekrönt, dahinter befindet sich das aus kostbarem Holz angefertigte Gestühl. Spärliches Licht fällt auf die Gemälde von Jacopo Tintoretto. Eine räumliche Inszenierung, die mich zugleich erhaben wie klein fühlen lässt. Im Klosterbereich hängt Vittore Carpaccios wunderbarer San Giorgio, der den Drachen tötet.
Zwischen meinen Arbeitsstunden freue ich mich auf das Mittagessen mit den Mönchen, sie kochen hervorragend und wir speisen im Refektorium, wo wir nebeneinander sitzend dem vorlesenden Ordensmann zuhören. Hinter dem Kloster halten die Mönche Hühner. Der Hahn heißt, wie könnte es anders sein, Tintoretto.

Mariendom Maria, Königin des Friedens
Neviges, Deutschland
Franziskanerorden ♂
Gebaut 1966–1968
Architekt Gottfried Böhm (geb. 1920)
Aufenthalt Januar 2013
Seite 30 Transept 13
Seite 41 Transept 16
Seite 44 KDF 1
Seite 43 KDF 3
Seite 47 KDF 4

Mächtig erhebt sich der Mariendom über den Ort Neviges. An riesige Steinblöcke erinnert seine Form, auch die expressionistischen Linien und Flächen von Lyonel Feininger kommen mir in den Sinn. Betritt man das Bauwerk, braucht es ein wenig, bis sich das Auge an die Dunkelheit gewöhnt. Nach und nach erscheint der von Gottfried Böhm entworfene Kirchenraum wie eine sakrale Stadt aus Sichtbeton. Das Licht dringt mal punktuell, mal flächig durch Fenster, die der Architekt ebenfalls entworfen hat. Ihr kräftiges Rot überstrahlt das Grau des Betons, bei starkem Sonnenlicht scheint er förmlich zu glühen. Immer wieder fallen mir junge Menschen auf, die sich vor den Altar auf den Boden legen. Beten im Brutalismus.

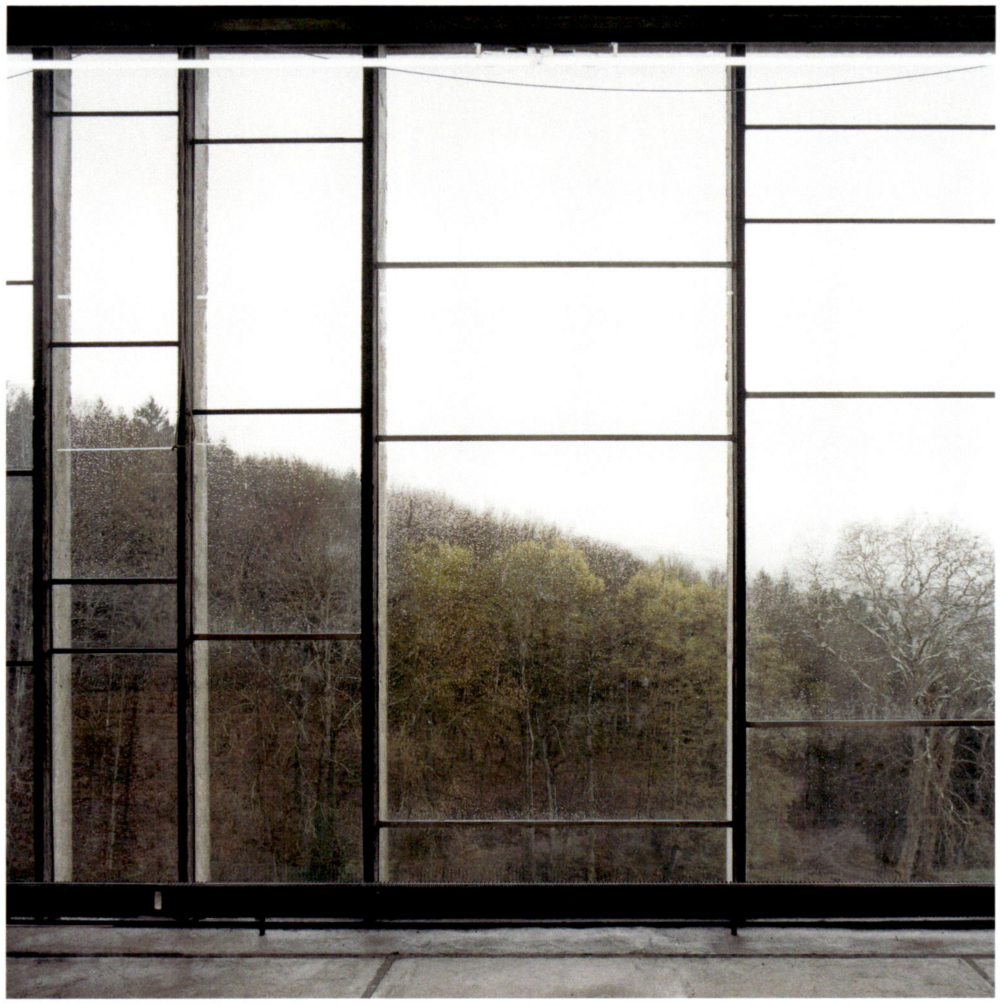

für Irene

special thanks to / besonderen Dank an:

Jutta Freifrau von Falkenhausen

the religious orders of /
die Ordensgemeinschaften von

Couvent Sainte-Marie de La Tourette
Abdij Roosenberg
Karmel Regina Martyrum
Abbazia di San Giorgio Maggiore
Mariendom Neviges

and / sowie
Giulio Bono
Frère Marc Chauveau
Gallery Fifty One
Esther Gallodoro
Daniel Ginelli
Carmelo Grasso
Theresa Hartherz
Birgit Möckel
Susanne Rösler
Sammlung SWW
Tas Skorupa
Tom Thys
Caroline Voet

Colophon / Impressum

Cover / Umschlagmotiv: Friederike von Rauch, Maria RM 10

Translation / Übersetzung „La lumière à La Tourette": Esther Gallodoro (German / Deutsch), John Tittensor, Lyon (English / Englisch)

Copyediting / Lektorat: Theresa Hartherz, jovis (German / Deutsch), Tas Skorupa, Berlin (English / Englisch)

Design and typesetting / Gestaltung und Satz: Susanne Rösler, jovis

Reproductions / Lithografie: Carsten Humme, Leipzig

Printing and binding / Druck und Bindung: Grafisches Centrum Cuno, Calbe

Bibliographic information published by the Deutsche Nationalbibliothek
The Deutsche Nationalbibliothek lists this publication in the Deutsche Nationalbibliografie; detailed bibliographic data are available on the internet at http://dnb.d-nb.de
Bibliografische Information der Deutschen Nationalbibliothek
Die Deutsche Nationalbibliothek verzeichnet diese Publikation in der Deutschen Nationalbibliografie; detaillierte bibliografische Daten sind im Internet über http://dnb.d-nb.de abrufbar.

jovis Verlag GmbH
Kurfürstenstraße 15/16
10785 Berlin

www.jovis.de

jovis books are available worldwide in select bookstores. Please contact your nearest bookseller or visit www.jovis.de for information concerning your local distribution.
jovis-Bücher sind weltweit im ausgewählten Buchhandel erhältlich. Informationen zu unserem internationalen Vertrieb erhalten Sie von Ihrem Buchhändler oder unter www.jovis.de.

ISBN 978-3-86859-591-8